MURDEROUS WOMEN

CONTENTS

PROLOGUE:
NO ORDINARY WOMEN

I remember one evening, as we sat talking in her little gamekeeper's cottage in Hay-On-Wye, asking author Kate Clarke what it is that fascinates her about women murderers.

Kate, who had just published, *The Pimlico Murder*, an account of the Adelaide Bartlett poison case, replied: 'I am interested in women who murder men. Not gory murders,' she added quickly. 'But sometimes women are put on the spot, and the only way out is cunning. They are desperate, and the only alternative seems to be murder. I'm never surprised at murder really,' she said. And with a laugh: 'I'm surprised only that there aren't more murders.'

Her comments pretty much explain why I, too, have been fascinated with women murderers over two decades and through the course of two previous books, why I find so much interest in visiting the places where these crimes occurred and exploring the lives and motives of these women. It isn't because I'm blood-thirsty — I am counted a fond grandfather. Rather, it's the human equation that intrigues me, and, above all, that old nagging question: why does one woman, finding herself in an odious and difficult situation, resort to murder while ten thousand other women, facing the same circumstances, do not?

Murder, of course, is nearly always fascinating, if for no other reason than that it is so final, so irrevocable. But women murderers are particularly interesting, first, because they are comparatively rare. In the United States, women are responsible for only 12 per cent of the killings, in Canada, 15 per cent (although my friend, State University of New York sociologist Gerhard Falk, believes that, because women have almost exclusive care of the very young and the very old, they get away with murder more often than is believed). Not being as strong as men, women historically have had to resort to more interesting and devious ways of killing, although that is not as true today, when handguns are more generally available, as it once was.

Men, of course, are more overtly violent; they kill their spouses and children in outbursts of anger, and often they murder strangers – in drunken brawls or in the commission of another crime, such as robbery. But murder by a woman is an intimate crime and creates a special kind of horror and a particular fascination.

One question I have had to take into consideration in selecting the cases and writing this book is the amazing 180-degree change that has occurred in society's – and writers' – attitudes toward women murderers. At one time, women murderers were regarded as freaks, and their study almost a branch of demonology. Even a woman writer, F. Tennyson Jesse, novelist and editor of

MURDEROUS WOMEN

True Tales of Women Who Killed

Frank Jones

HEADLINE

Copyright © 1991 Frank Jones

The right of Frank Jones to be identified as the Author of the Work has been asserted by him in accordance with the Copyright, Designs and Patents Act 1988.

First published in Canada by
Key Porter Books Limited, Toronto

First published in Great Britain in 1991
by HEADLINE BOOK PUBLISHING PLC

10 9 8 7 6 5 4 3 2 1

British Library Cataloguing in Publication Data

Jones, Frank
Murderous women.
I. Title
364.15230922

ISBN 0-7472-0505-1

Typeset by Medcalf Type Ltd, Bicester, Oxon

Printed and bound in Great Britain by
Richard Clay Ltd, Bungay, Suffolk

HEADLINE BOOK PUBLISHING PLC
Headline House
79 Great Titchfield Street
London W1P 7FN

numerous of the Notable British Trials volumes, could write that the woman murderer 'can be more cruel in vengeance, more relentless in pursuit, and more utterly conscienceless.' The woman criminal, she said in her 1924 opus, *Murder and Its Motives*, 'is the panther of the underworld. She can follow relentlessly through the jungle day after day, she can wait her time, she can play with her victim and torture him in sheer wantonness, and she can pile cruelty upon the act of killing as does the panther, but never the lion.'

Today, when we are more familiar with the plight of the abused wife, and when the ravages of rapists, child murderers and serial killers, all male, dominate the headlines, such generalizations seem so much poppycock.

Recognizing that the majority of women murderers are only striking out at the men who beat them (90 per cent of victims of female killers in the United States are men), we've swung right around, regarding female killers almost invariably as victims. 'Women who kill,' writes Ann Jones in her book of that title, 'find extreme solutions to problems that thousands of women cope with in more peaceable ways from day to day.' But why them? Why do these particular women pick up a gun or a knife, go to the poison cabinet, when others don't? While I don't subscribe to the old-fashioned 'woman as devil' theory, neither do I support British novelist and poet Enid Bagnold's flat statement: 'A murderess is only an ordinary woman in a temper.'

A lot of that has to do with my two year personal involvement with the case of a native Canadian woman named Khristine Linklater, a one-time member of the

Northwest Territories cross-country ski team. In March
1979, Khristine was found guilty of the murder of her
husband, William, in Old Crow, a tiny community on
the shores of the Beaufort Sea in the Arctic. Her
conviction, and the imposition of a life sentence to be
served in Canada's only women's penitentiary, in
Kingston, 3,000 miles away from her home and her baby
son, had aroused indignation in the Yukon, where the
trial had taken place. Evidence showed that, after an all-
night drinking session and after being abused once too
often, she had grabbed a high-powered rifle from the wall
of their home, followed William, and shot him down as
he walked across the community airstrip.

I flew to Whitehorse for the *Toronto Star* and, with
the help of the wife of a Yukon cabinet minister, gained
admission to the correctional centre; there I met Khristine
in the prison laundry, feeling very sorry for herself. Before
the trial, she told me, one of William's brothers had
visited her in prison, telling her that if she bad-mouthed
her late husband in court, his brothers would fix her when
she got back to Old Crow. With William's four brothers
glaring at her in court, she had sat almost mute in the
witness box, unwilling to tell how, for example, William
had knocked her down in the street one day when she
was pregnant and kicked her. The usual verdict in such
cases, which are all too frequent in the North, is 'guilty
of manslaughter.' A gasp went through the courtroom
when the all-white jury found Khristine guilty of murder.

About a week later, after my article on the case had
appeared, I was having dinner at the Toronto home of
a woman known for her good works when she brought

up the subject of Khristine. Something should be done for her, she said. Before I knew it, I was on the phone to Khristine's appeal lawyer, Paul O'Brien, explaining that, if Khristine could get bail, she would be given the air fare to Toronto, where my friend would also pay for her to receive treatment in the Donwood Institute, a highly regarded addiction treatment centre.

I went on vacation to England at that point, returning to discover that the judge had granted Khristine bail so that she could come to Toronto. And, not having the name of anyone else who could be responsible, he had appointed me, in effect, as her guardian. She was arriving on a plane the next day.

Khristine stayed with our family for several weeks before moving to the Donwood Institute. There she quickly impressed the staff with her ability and enthusiasm, and was soon helping with organizational tasks. It would be two years before Khristine's appeal was heard, and wherever she went it was always the same story: she was cheerful, engaging and hard-working. She became involved in the native spiritual movement, and wrote quite beautiful poems, which she signed 'Springflower.'

It was one of the most thrilling moments of my life when I drove out to the correctional centre in Toronto, where she had been detained while the actual appeal was heard, to inform her that the justices had wiped out the murder conviction and substituted a verdict of manslaughter. The staff as well as the inmates were cheering for Khristine. A few weeks later, when she was back in court in Whitehorse for resentencing, I was one of many witnesses who testified to the way she had turned her life around; it was almost like a graduation as the judge gave her a suspended sentence. While her supporters crowded around, congratulating her, I slipped away to catch my plane south. I was at the check-in counter at the airport when I heard a familiar laugh. Khristine was there with Paul O'Brien to say goodbye, and I don't expect ever to see a bigger smile on any woman's face.

Khristine returned to Fort McPherson, the northern town where she'd grown up, with dreams of becoming an alcohol-addiction counsellor. But eighteen months later she was back in court, sentenced to sixteen months in jail for assaulting a woman, causing bodily harm. Later she was returned to Whitehorse, where, having breached the conditions of her suspended sentence, she was given a three-year term for the original manslaughter conviction.

It would be easy to say that Khristine came from a culture of violence where alcohol has broken down all restraints. It would be easy to say that, when she killed William, she was reacting as any woman pushed to the limit would. But, for every woman who kills her violent husband, thousands of others either put up with abuse or leave; of all the thousands of girls brought up, as Khristine was, in foster homes and in a society ruined by drink, only a very few eventually turn to violence. Reading the poems Khristine gave me, I admire her sensitivity and her fresh, wondering approach to nature. But I know there is another Khristine, the woman who did not, in fact, shoot her husband in blind retaliation for a blow, but let her anger simmer and then, having decided to act, stalked him and shot him, as she would a caribou. And the tragedy of Khristine is that, while she had so much ability, so much ambition, so much to give her own people, she was also one of those very rare women who could kill.

The same is true of some — though not all — of the women I have written about here, any one of whom would provide the raw material for a novel. Some, like the gauzy Alma Rattenbury or the malleable Katie Harper, almost drifted into murder in a mood of forgetfulness. Others, such as Elizabeth Jones living out big-screen fantasies of gangster life, and Louise Masset, hoping the death of a child would bring her marital bliss, were victims of self-delusion. There are others though who would please F. Tennyson Jesse, such women as Madame Fahmy and the bold Clara Ford who, perhaps provoked, nevertheless stalked their prey. Above all, there is Myra Hindley, always there to challenge any preconceptions we might have about the nature of violence in women.

Before the transformation that sudden notoriety brings, Hindley going to her office job in Manchester, Christiana Edmunds walking the sea front at Brighton, even Jean Harris dealing with the day-to-day trivia of her job as headmistress, might have seemed to be ordinary enough women living humdrum lives. Only when violence intruded did they become extraordinary.

Ultimately, of course, their motives, their innermost thoughts, are unknowable. The extent to which they were pushed by intolerable circumstances or pulled by a natural propensity for violence is a matter of conjecture. Whatever the equation, the stories of these women form an irresistibly intriguing chapter in the human experience and leave us with only one certainty: that these were no ordinary women.

THE
GANGSTER'S MOLL

It was more real when the lights went down. The big Wurlitzer sank into the pit, she showed the last few stragglers to their seats with her flashlight, and then the MGM lion was roaring up on the screen or the glittering CBS statuette was holding up her torch. Leaning on the barrier at the back, lost in the darkness, she could be herself. 'Coming out for a fag?' the other girls would ask her. 'No thanks, I'm fine here.' 'How many times can you watch that thing? Got a crush on Humphrey Bogart, have you?' And they'd go out giggling.

Oh, sometimes she'd join them if it was just one of those silly films about pirates or if it was only a Western. But not when it was Edward G. Robinson. Or George Raft. Or Humphrey Bogart. And no, it wasn't because Betty Jones was stuck on those male stars in the gangster movies. It was the women she watched. The molls.

Broads, that's what their men called them. Her mother would call them brassy sluts, but what did she know? Betty Jones could see that, up there on the screen, women were living the kind of life she wanted for herself, not

1

caring what people thought, not having to smile and be nice and soft all the time, not minding guns and blood and even a slap in the face now and then. Whatever happened, those women could curl a lip, just like Joan Crawford, and spit in someone's face.

If you were a woman like that you wouldn't have to worry about some dirty old bugger catching you in the bicycle shed and getting his hand in your knickers, and you thirteen and shouting, 'Don't, don't, please,' and his breath coming in your ear, panting, 'Keep still; keep still now, love; it' ll be over in a minute.' And your dad saying, 'Shut your dirty little mouth, Betty. Dan Edwards is my friend. He would never do anything like that. Go to your room, you little liar.' Oh Dad, Dad, I loved you so much.

'Miss Jones! Really, Miss Jones! These people have been waiting to be shown to their seats for some time. Please come and see me in my office afterwards.'

Later, with the little envelope containing what they owed her at the cinema in her pocket, she took the bus home, the searchlights sweeping the sky above Chelsea, then climbed the stairs to her one-room flat at the top of the house in Hammersmith. Tomorrow she'd think about getting another job, but not now. Now she got out her writing paper and the lists of addresses she'd sent away to the studios for.

'Dear Miss Crawford, My name is . . .' She couldn't use a silly old name like Betty Jones, or even her proper name, Elizabeth Maude Jones. Joan Crawford would only laugh and throw away her letter. 'My name is Georgina Grayson. I am eighteen and I trained as a dancer at . . .' Better not to tell her where she'd trained. Doesn't sound good: 'Georgina Grayson learned to dance at a reform school in Manchester to which she was sent after running away from home repeatedly.' Betty had to smile. 'I trained at one of the best dancing schools in England and I have fulfilled several engagements at some top London clubs.' Top London clubs! The Panama Club in Knightsbridge and the Blue Lagoon Club on Carnaby Street? Dives, you'd have to call them. And it wasn't really dancing she did. It was stripping, and she lasted only a few nights at both places. One time a bunch of drunken British soldiers had laughed her off the stage.

'I have always admired you so much, Miss Crawford. I know I have a big future in Hollywood if only I can get a start. Could you please put a word in for me? I would be so grateful . . .'

As she sealed the envelope, she checked the loudly ticking tin alarm clock on the dressing table. It was still early − only ten o'clock. Plenty of time to go to the Blue Spot Cafe for a bite. Who knows, she might meet a new Yank!

It was October 3, 1944, and Americans were everywhere. As the war in Europe entered its final phase, 1.5 million GIs were in peaceful occupation of Britain − in the pubs, in the night clubs and on the streets. On virtually any British thoroughfare, U.S. servicemen were followed like Pied Pipers by children crying, 'Got any gum, chum?'

Politicians in Britain feared that the huge American influx would create bad feeling and, ultimately, outbreaks of violence. But, almost invariably, the GIs were polite, friendly and downright irresistible, and beyond some pub brawling and inevitable resentments when British girls threw over local sweethearts for the glamorous Yanks, the invasion turned into a love-in.

For Betty Jones, who had run away to London, leaving her parents' home in Neath, in Wales, two years earlier, when she was sixteen, the American presence was the next-best thing to her Hollywood idols stepping down off the screen. Yanks became her obsession.

She kept a list of the American officers with whom she'd been out, carefully noting down their ranks, nicknames and home towns, adding beside some names 'missing' or 'shot down.' She supposed the war was tragic and all that, and she never forgot that her dad was a soldier too, but, if truth be told, she'd never had so much in her life and never expected to again. The blackout, the air-raid sirens, the young men in their snazzy American uniforms who might be gone forever tomorrow . . . This was living.

'Georgina! Thought you were working tonight.' Her friend, Beryl, waited on tables at the Blue Spot.

'Got the sack. The manager caught me day-dreaming.

'Oh, what a shame. What will you do?'

'I don't care. I still get my husband's army allowance. Even though I haven't seen him in a couple of years.' Husband! That was a joke. He was thirteen years older than she and already in the paratroopers when her parents pressured her into marrying him. Thought it would take the wildness out of her, she supposed now. But he hit her the night they were married, and she cleared off and never saw him again.

'Come and sit down here, love,' Beryl's father called,

patting the chair beside him. Betty ('Georgina' in this chapter of her life) had met him several times before. 'Call me Len,' he'd said the first time they'd met, and just a little she envied Beryl having a father who was always around and who was so easy-going. 'Can I order you chop and chips? This is Ricky. He's on leave and all on his lonesome.

She took in, first, the American lieutenant's stripes and then the face – boyish features, hardly set, yet with a firmness about the mouth.

'Georgina, was it? I'm mighty pleased to meet you.' His voice was stronger, louder than she'd expected. His hand was large and hardened, as if he was used to wielding machinery or tools. 'Can I call you Georgie?'

'Georgina will suit me very nicely, if you don't mind. Where are you stationed, Ricky?'

'Just got back from Holland. We're not properly settled yet. Say, did I hear an American accent there?'

'No.' She laughed, and blushed. 'If it's anything, it's Canadian. I spent five years there with my parents when I was small. Then we came back to Wales just before the war started.'

'And what do you do, Georgina?'

'I'm a show girl,' she said without hesitation. 'You know, I dance at different clubs.'

By the time the food came, Len, sitting beside them, was forgotten.

'How would you like to go out for a drive, baby?' Ricky asked her after they'd eaten.

'It's half-past eleven,' she said. 'Don't you have to be back?'

5

'Don't worry about it. Look, I'll see you in about ten minutes outside that movie theatre up the street. What's it called?'

'The Broadway Cinema?'

'That's it. The Broadway.'

But he didn't come. She'd freshened up and put on a new coat of lipstick in the ladies', and he'd left her standing there. After ten minutes, she started to walk home.

'Georgina! Georgina!'

She couldn't see where the voice was coming from. The street was empty except for a huge, ten-wheeled American Army truck.

'Up here, Georgina!' He was grinning at the surprised expression on her face. 'Come on up. I'll open the passenger door for you.'

She didn't ask him why an officer was driving a truck. There was something about Ricky that said you didn't ask him things like that.

'How say we take a drive to Reading?' he said, naming a town some thirty miles west of London. 'Do you mind?' She shook her head. 'What do you want to do, baby? Any ideas?' he asked as he swung the truck expertly through a traffic roundabout.

Ideas? She leaned back, resting her head against the back of the seat. 'Oh, I want to do something dangerous, Ricky.'

'Dangerous?'

'Yah, like fly over Germany on a bombing mission. Can you arrange that?'

In the darkness she could see his white teeth gleaming.

'I can arrange something better than that. Here.' He was pulling something out from his belt. She had never in real life seen a revolver, but as he handed it to her she recognized the feel.

'It's so heavy.'

'You bet. We don't use toys where I come from.'

'Where's that?'

'Chicago. I ran with the mob there.'

'You were . . . a gunman?' She made no attempt to keep the excitement out of her voice. 'Honestly?'

'Honest to god. You scared?'

She felt laughter welling up. 'Does that make me a, you know, gun moll?'

She could sense his smile. 'Anything you like, baby. And I may as well tell you − the truck, that's stolen.'

'I don't care. I don't care a bit, Ricky.'

They had left the Great West Road now, and the truck was rolling along a narrow, winding track on the outskirts of a village. Suddenly, by the dim lights of the hooded headlamps, Georgina saw the outline of a cyclist ahead. A moment later she could see it was a woman who seemed to be in uniform. 'Watch out, Ricky, you'll hit her!' she cried, but too late. The bike spun crazily down the road under its own volition until the woman was pitched into the ditch. Georgina was shaking. 'Didn't you see her?'

'Sure I saw her. Now be a good girl and come and help me.'

She was still trembling as she got down from the truck. 'Ricky, is she . . . did you . . .?'

'Kill her? Do ya think I'm stupid!' He was bending over the twisted bicycle. 'The dame's run off. See, she wasn't

7

even hurt. But she left her pocket-book behind. Here.' He threw it to her. 'We better get going.'

On the way back to London, Georgina used her flashlight to search the pocket-book. The woman's ID papers showed she was a WAAF. 'There's five shillings here,' she said, 'and some clothing coupons.' He told her to keep the money and give him the coupons (used during the war to buy strictly rationed new clothing) because he could sell them on the black market. The sky was beginning to lighten when Ricky dropped her off at 311 King Street in Hammersmith. Climbing the stairs to her room, she felt light-headed. This was it, wasn't it, what she'd been waiting for? On the way back to town Ricky had told her he was the leader of a gang in London. 'My guys will be watching you, so you better not make a wrong move,' he'd warned her as she climbed down. He didn't need to say that. She'd be there, waiting for him.

That day she didn't go out, except to get her meals at the cafe next door. She made sure to get a table by the window so she could see if he came. But it wasn't until the next day, a Thursday, that he turned up, late in the afternoon, and Len Bexley, Beryl's father, was with him.

'Let's go to a movie, honey. Would you like that?' It seemed odd, the three of them going together, but she didn't object. The movie was *The Last Gangster*, and it starred Preston Foster as one of Al Capone's sidekicks. Lois Andrews played his girl. Ricky held her hand and, at the part where the FBI had Foster trapped with all guns blazing, he moved her hand so she could feel the bulk of the gun in his belt. It was kind of a joke, like that was make-believe on the screen, but real life at the same time.

8

THE GANGSTER'S MOLL

Afterwards, saying goodnight to Len, they were going into a cafe on Hammersmith Broadway when the air-raid siren sounded. 'We won't get served now,' said Ricky as the few customers in the place headed for the underground station. 'Come on.' In the cinema parking lot, the truck loomed out of the darkness like some dumb, patient monster. Ricky said he was going to rob a pub, but after stopping outside one place for a few minutes he drove off again.

'Why did you do that?' she asked.

'We were being watched,' he said shortly.

'Why don't you rob a cab?' she suggested as they swung around Marble Arch. 'Look, that one there.'

They followed the cab until they came to a quiet street in Cricklewood and Ricky felt it was safe to overtake it and cut off the other driver. He was waving the gun as he jumped down and ran over to the car, but a few moments later he climbed back in and gunned the engine. 'That was a close thing,' he said. 'There was an American army officer in the back. He had his gun out.'

They were driving along the Edgware Road when Georgina told him to stop. 'There was a girl back there. Let's back up.' The girl, who was maybe nineteen, was carrying two suitcases tied with rope.

'Where you going, honey?' Ricky asked.

She peered up suspiciously at him, then, seeing Georgina, she relaxed. 'Paddington. I'm catching the train to Bristol. I'm not sure I'll make it.'

'We're going to Reading. We could give you a lift and you could catch your train from there. I'll put your valises in the back.'

The girl, who said her name was Violet Hodge, climbed in and sat between them. Soon she was chattering away, telling them about her job waitressing in London and her plans for when she got home to Bristol. They were passing Runnymede Park beside the River Thames when Ricky exclaimed, 'Aw shit,' and pulled off the road.

'What's the matter?' asked Georgina.

'I think it's a flat tire.' All three got out. 'Get her with her back to me,' he said under his breath to Georgina.

'Want a fag?' she asked the girl, and lit it for her, bracing herself for the expected impact. It didn't come.

'Georgina,' he said, 'will you hop in the back and get me some blocks?' She could see the girl looking up into the back of the truck as Ricky moved in behind her. The crack as the iron bar came down on the girl's head made Georgina catch her breath, but Violet didn't go down. Ricky had her by the throat, and then she fell forward on her face and he was kneeling on her back. 'Help me, for chrissake,' he gasped. 'Grab that arm.' Georgina put her knee on Violet's flailing arm while her fingers explored her coat pockets.

Then the girl was still.

'Only five bob!' said Georgina in disgust.

'There's the suitcases,' said Ricky. 'And help me get her coat off.'

'We can't leave her here. She'll be found,' she said.

'Grab her feet,' he told her. Hanging limply between them, Violet seemed to weigh a ton. Georgina's heart was pounding by the time they reached the riverbank. They didn't have the strength to throw her in, but just sort of slid her in, as if they were launching a boat, then hurried back to the truck.

This time, when they got back to her place, Ricky came up. 'You've got blood on your trousers,' she said after she'd hung the clothing from the suitcases in her closet. 'And look, there's dark stains on your leather jacket.'

'I'll look after it in the morning, baby,' he said.

It was afternoon when they woke. 'Do me a favour, honey,' he said as she came out of the bathroom. 'Fetch my valise from the station. Here, I've got the cloakroom ticket.' Half an hour later she was back with the suitcase from the left-luggage office at Hammersmith Metropolitan Station. Ricky opened it and took out a pair of dark pants, which he put on. Beneath them in the suitcase were two long, deadly-looking daggers. 'Here, you hold it like this,' he said, putting one in her hand. 'Now you bring it up, like so.' Soon after, he went out, saying he'd be back in a couple of hours.

But it was 11:30 p.m. when she heard his whistle in the street below.

The following morning, Saturday, October 7, Robert Balding, an auxiliary fireman, came off duty in Staines, twenty miles west of London, at nine o'clock and, as usual, took a short cut home, across Knowle Green. Something dark caught his attention in the ditch. Stopping, he saw that it was the figure of a man, the collar of his blue overcoat pulled up over his face. 'I thought he had been taken ill and had lain down,' said Balding later. But, when he shook the man, he realized he was dead. Police found the tire marks of a large

11

vehicle on the grass nearby. The man had died from a single bullet wound in the back.

Earlier that morning, not far away, an electrician's apprentice had found a wallet beside the road, containing an identity card and a driving licence belonging to a thirty-four-year-old private-hire car driver named George Heath.

Considering that thousands of men, women and children were at that time losing their lives in the bombing and artillery fire, the murder of George Heath prompted a surprising reaction in the London press. As the details emerged, the demise of Heath, who had been a soldier at the Dunkirk evacuation and who had only recently recovered from civilian bomb injuries, pushed major war stories off front pages. Initially, because Heath had ink on his hands, the case was called 'The Inky Fingers Murder.' Later, when photographs showed Heath had a dimple in his chin, even the august *Times* called it 'The Cleft Chin Murder.'

Police immediately issued a description of Heath's Ford V8 car, licence number RD8955, which had gone missing. Two days later, a constable noticed it parked in front of a house on Fulham Palace Road. When, forty-five minutes later, an American Army lieutenant came out of the house and got into the car, a constable grabbed his wrist and asked, 'Is this your car, sir?' When the man didn't answer, the policeman shouted, the headlights of a police car parked nearby flashed on, and other officers charged to his assistance. In the man's pocket was an automatic pistol, loaded, and with the safety catch off.

12

Thus ended the brief freedom fling of Karl Gustav Hulten, a private with the 2nd battalion of the 501st Parachute Infantry Regiment, who sometimes went by the name 'Rick Allen' and who had deserted his regiment late in August, taking with him a truck and an automatic pistol. Hulten's story, related to Lieutenant Robert De Mott, a lawyer with the American Army CID, was that he had simply found the Ford V8 abandoned the previous day. He had spent the night of the murder with a girl called Georgina Grayson at her place in Hammersmith. He even offered to show the police where she lived.

When they arrived at 311 King Street that afternoon, they found Georgina in bed. At the station, 'Georgina' owned up to being Elizabeth Marina Jones (she would not admit to 'Maude' as a middle name until she was actually in court), and, yes, she had met the man she knew as Ricky at the Blue Spot Cafe. He had spent the evening elsewhere, but from 11:30 on the night of the murder he had been at her flat. Jones was allowed to go.

And, apart, perhaps, from appearing as a witness in Hulten's trial, nothing more would have been heard of the gun moll – if she hadn't told an acquaintance, a war reserve policeman who noticed how ill she looked, 'If you had seen somebody do what I have seen done, you wouldn't be able to sleep at night.'

In no time she was back at the police station, giving Detective Inspector Bert Tansell her account of that night's events: her account, because from here on Jones and Hulten were each to tell a very different version.

When she'd come downstairs in answer to his whistle, she said, Hulten had told her, 'Come on, let's go and get a taxi.' By that, he meant rob a cab driver, she explained. They stood in a shop doorway until they saw a grey Ford approaching slowly, as a cab would. 'Taxi!' Jones cried. Hulten, fearing it was a Navy car, hung back while she went and spoke to the driver. Heath had told her he was a hire car, which meant he wasn't supposed to cruise for passengers. How much would it be to take them to the top of King Street? Ten shillings, said Heath, naming an exorbitant price for what was only a short trip. Hulten and Jones had no reason to quibble: they didn't expect to pay.

'We've passed King Street,' Heath, thin-faced with a Cockney's sharp, street-sparrow eyes, said. 'Where do you want to go?'

'It's farther on. I don't mind paying more,' said the American. Heath happily complied. As they entered the Great West Road, Jones saw that Hulten, sitting directly behind the driver, had his gun out. 'Go slowly,' he told Heath, and a few minutes later, 'We'll get out here.'

Heath leaned back with the intention of opening the rear door on her side of the car. Jones saw a flash, and was stunned by the noise in the confined space. As the driver moaned, Hulten leaped out and got behind the wheel. 'Move over,' he said, shoving Heath into the passenger seat, 'or I'll give you another dose of the same.'

Suddenly the car was moving again. 'Tear down that window blind and see if anyone's following us,' ordered Hulten.

She pulled up a corner of the blind on the back window. 'Nobody,' she said.

'Go through the guy's pockets.' She leaned over the front seat. Heath was gasping. His wallet wasn't in his inside pocket. Finally, struggling to reach, she found it in his left-hand overcoat pocket. Inside was four pounds (twenty dollars) and a photograph. From other pockets she took his identity papers, his change, a silver cigarette case and lighter, a fountain pen and a silver pencil.

'Does he have a watch?' asked Hulten, driving fast now. She ran her hand down Heath's arm, found the wristwatch and handed it to him. 'Look on the floor for the bullet,' he ordered her. She searched with her flashlight, but didn't find it.

Hulten drove the big Ford on to some sort of open ground. 'He got out,' Jones told the police, 'and dragged the body from the car and rolled it into the ditch.' There was blood on his hands when he got back in, and she handed him Heath's handkerchief to wipe himself.

'Watch out for fingerprints,' he said, as she got into the front seat.

They set off for London, and this time Jones found the bullet casing, throwing it out of the window along with Heath's ID papers. Hulten parked in the cinema lot behind Hammersmith Broadway: they wiped the car clean of fingerprints and went for a bite. The cafe was full of cab drivers. Oddly, when Jones and Hulten asked for someone to drive them home after, no one would.

'He's dead, isn't he?' Jones said she asked him as they arrived home. He nodded. 'That's cold-blooded murder then. How could you do it?'

15

'People in my profession,' said the Chicago gunman, 'haven't the time to think what they do.'

Karl Hulten, aged twenty-two, was born in Stockholm, taken to America as a child and brought up, not on the rough side of Chicago, but in genteel Cambridge, Massachusetts, in the shadow of Harvard University. He had never until then been in trouble with the law, he said, but admitted he had once 'passed through' Chicago; under the relentless questioning of Lieutenant De Mott, Hulten agreed that Jones's story was essentially accurate. It was only on the description of her role in the affair that he differed.

He hadn't wanted to rob a cab driver that night at all, he insisted. It was Jones who had argued they should. When he refused, she'd told him to give her the gun and she'd do it herself. Taken in a police car to the spot where the body was found, he said, 'I wouldn't have been here but for the girl. I wanted to go for a walk, but she didn't want to.'

As police drove her to Staines to formally charge her with Heath's murder, Jones, as they entered the Great West Road, said. 'That's where he shot him.'

The Hulten–Jones case made headlines on both sides of the Atlantic, if only because it was the severest breach yet in the touchy relations between U.S. military forces and the British civilian population. That Betty Jones had seen herself as a Chicago-style gun moll only confirmed suspicions about the unfortunate effects the American influence was having on the British lifestyle; in Germany, Hitler's radio service broadcast gleeful reports on the case.

Under the Visiting Forces Act of 1942, Hulten would

have been tried by an American Army tribunal. Indeed, many Americans felt it would be wrong to hand him over to the British courts. But there was an ally to be appeased, and a few days after he was re-elected to a fourth term, on November 7, President Franklin D. Roosevelt agreed to waive rights under the act, leaving the job to the British courts.

When Betty Jones and Karl Hulten were led into the dock at the Old Bailey on January 16, 1945, the dozens of British and American journalists covering the trial found it hard to reconcile the two drab figures with the glamorous 'Chicago gunman' and 'striptease dancer' of the headlines. Hulten, pasty-faced, dark-haired, with a receding hairline, looked just what he was: a nervous young soldier in uniform and greatcoat. The gun moll and strip dancer, after a couple of months in Holloway Prison, was deathly pale, a slight and pathetic figure who wouldn't have earned a second glance on the street. Her one distinction was a dubious one: she was the first female accused ever to appear at the Old Bailey hatless.

The two had fed on each other's fantasies, each seeing in the other a reflection, if only a dim one, of the glamorous gangland figures portrayed in the movies. Now, facing the death penalty if convicted, each tried to blame the other.

Jones, perhaps after a word in her ear from her solicitor, had laid the groundwork for her defence in a letter written to Hulten from Holloway. 'Dear Ricky,' it began. Her mother, she said, was 'breaking her heart over me. If I should get sent to prison − convicted − it will kill her . . . You must tell the truth, Ricky. What

17

the police have against me is going through the man's pockets. Had you not ordered me to do so, I would never have done it, but as my own life was in danger I did so . . . I did not help you to carry him to the ditch. You know that, Ricky. For God's sake tell the truth.' And this time when she signed, it was not 'Georgina' but simply 'Georgie.'

Her theme would be that she had acted in terror of Hulten. But when Len Bexley, who admitted buying some of George Heath's possessions from Hulten, was asked in court what her attitude had been toward Hulten, he replied, 'I should say very intimate.' What did he mean by that? 'Very fond,' said Bexley.

Going into the witness box, Betty Jones seemed scared out of her wits. But, wrote C.E. Beechhoffer Roberts in the foreword to the official trial transcript, 'a curious change could be seen in her during the hours she spent in the witness box. Colour gradually crept back into her cheeks; her voice, at first nearly inaudible, became stronger; and at moments she showed glimpses of the vitality and good looks which she had formerly possessed. Perhaps she was a girl who "lived a part" as an actress does: telling the story of her six days' career as a "gun moll" may have made her unconsciously recover some of its thrills and excitement.'

She gave her age as eighteen. 'Eighteen years and seven months, isn't it?' said the judge. In Britain, at that time, people under the age of eighteen were not hanged. The judge wanted there to be no doubt that she was a candidate for the noose.

Jones, whose parents were in court, described growing

18

up resentful that her mother devoted most of her love and attention to her invalid sister, Gladys. There was the trauma of the sexual assault by an older man, a friend of her parents, and the burning anger when her parents refused to believe her. Soon afterwards her father was called up, and Jones ran away from home three times to find him. After that, it was reform school, a one-night marriage at age sixteen, and, finally, a life of her own in London.

After she met Hulten, she claimed, she went in fear of him. He had several times threatened her with his gun and two daggers, slapped her once when she left the apartment without his permission and warned her frequently that his people were watching her. After he shot Heath, she said, she refused at first when he told her to search his pockets.

'What happened then?' asked prosecution counsel.

'So Ricky picked up the revolver that was lying on the seat and said, "You heard what I said. I can easy do the same to you." '

The day after the murder, she said, she had gone to a dog-racing track and the cinema with Hulten.

'With the man you knew to be a murderer?' said the judge disbelievingly.

'Ye-es,' she replied hesitantly.

When his turn came to testify, Hulten claimed he had only been holding the gun and that, as he went to get out of the car, his sleeve caught in the door and it went off by accident, killing Heath. At the end of the ride, 'Mrs Jones took his feet and helped carry him to where he was put in the ditch.' Police evidence, that there was no sign

19

the body had been dragged across the grass, tended to confirm his version.

The jury took only eighty minutes to find Hulten guilty, and Jones guilty with a recommendation for mercy. 'Lies, lies, all lies. Why don't you tell the truth?' Jones shrieked at her former accomplice after Mr. Justice Charles had condemned them both to death. Thus far, the jury had heard nothing of the couple's crime spree, apart from the murder of Heath. Now the judge informed jurors that, by their own statements, the couple had earlier been 'engaged in murderous and near-murderous attacks on other people' (Violet Hodge, fortunately, had been shocked back into consciousness by the freezing water after being thrown into the River Thames, and had crawled to a cottage nearby).

Controversy continued to dog the case. While some campaigned for Jones's reprieve on the grounds of her youth, 'Hang Jones' signs appeared in South Wales. George Bernard Shaw, in an inane letter to *The Times*, argued that such cases showed that hanging should be abolished in favour of 'state-contrived euthanasia' — whatever that meant. Heath's car was displayed by an opportunistic businessman on Oxford Street, complete with cut-out figures of Jones and Hulten.

Only two days short of the March 8, 1945, execution date, the government, with a cautious eye to American reaction, reprieved Jones, but not Hulten. She would remain in prison for nine years before being released at age twenty-seven. She never followed through on a prison vow to become a nun; instead, she married, and died a number of years ago.

In Cambridge, Massachusetts, a last-minute appeal from Hulten's young wife, Rita, to Franklin Roosevelt to intervene went unanswered. With a silent crowd of 500 standing outside, Karl Hulten was hanged at 9:00 a.m. on the execution day.

Deploring the fuss over the case, George Orwell in his essay 'Decline of the English Murder' would claim that modern murder was a crass affair, lacking the 'depth of feeling' of classic domestic crimes of such people as Dr. Crippen and Florence Maybrick. But, writing in 1946, perhaps Orwell lacked the perspective to see that, in trying to create their own gangster world in imitation of the movies, Hulten and Jones had acted out of a longing to transcend the ordinary, to be larger than life.

A SHOOTING
IN HAMPSTEAD

Betty Jones tried living out the glamorous life she saw
portrayed in gangster movies, and the movies eventually
returned the compliment: in 1990 the Jones–Hulten case
was the subject of a British film titled *Chicago Joe and
the Showgirl.*

In the same sort of symbiotic embrace between art
and life, the career of Ruth Ellis, a brassy London bar
girl who sought entry to the world of fast cars and fast
company, has provided fodder for the stage and screen.
Her crime, which some regarded as merely sordid at the
time, has inspired two movies, including the cult favourite
Dance with a Stranger, a play, a TV drama starring the
late Diana Dors, and three books. Like Jones, Ellis did
not live to see her life writ large: she was the last woman
to be hanged in Britain.

The Magdala Tavern in fashionable Hampstead, where
the murder occurred on a balmy Easter weekend in 1955,
is still there, although the front wall chipped by bullets
has long since been repaired. You can see the spot where
Ruth's twenty-five-year-old boyfriend, David Blakely,

23

a sallow young man who tried to conceal his character weaknesses behind the bravura front of a racing-car driver, parked his small station wagon that night before going into the saloon bar with his friend Clive Gunnell to buy cigarettes and beers. It was Easter Sunday, one of those mild evenings when Hampstead takes on an almost Parisian flair with couples strolling, dropping into the pub. Blakely cashed a cheque for five pounds with the landlord, had a drink at the bar, then bought three flagons of beer before heading back to the car. Juggling the bottles and trying to reach for the keys to the grey and green, two-tone Standard Vanguard, he apparently didn't notice the slight peroxide blonde in the dark-rimmed glasses walking down South Hill Park toward him.

He was concentrating on getting the car door open and not dropping the bottles, so much so that he didn't seem to notice when she called out, 'David!' When he looked up, his face, small chin, narrow, almost feminine features, registered surprise at seeing her standing beside him. There was no time for shock to set in. She opened her purse and took out the large Smith and Wesson .38 so quickly that the words – of greeting perhaps, but more likely of excuse – died on his lips. In that frozen instant, the gun looked impossibly large in her small, pale hands. As he turned to run, she fired, and then fired again. Momentum carried him to the back corner of the car. 'Clive!' he screamed. Ruth Ellis, still holding the gun out in front of her, came after him.

'Get out of the way, Clive,' she snapped. The gun shook as she fired toward Blakely's back while he

24

writhed, bleeding, on the ground, and one wild bullet hit a passer-by, Gladys Kensington Yule, in the thumb. Blakely was bleeding from the mouth, his blood mixing with the beer now frothing into the gutter. The firing stopped. All six bullets were spent. Her main regret at that moment, she would say, was that she had meant to save the last bullet for herself.

The crowd poured out of the pub. 'What have you done?' someone shouted. 'You'll both die now.' A tall man who had been having a drink in the bar and who, shortly before, had noticed the blonde peering through the window, stepped forward with an air of authority. 'Phone the police,' Ruth Ellis told him. 'I am a police officer,' he said. Off-duty constable Alan Thompson reached out and took the gun from her. She said nothing as they waited for police cars and an ambulance to arrive. At the police station, they offered her a cup of tea and a cigarette. Then, perfectly in control, she. said, 'My name is Mrs. Ruth Ellis. I am a model. I am twenty-eight and I live at 44 Egerton Gardens, that's Kensington.' Charged later, she said, 'I am guilty. I am rather confused.'

There was nothing immortal, nothing elevating about the affair between Ruth Ellis and David Blakely. You couldn't properly call it a romance. It was more a grasping for control, an out-of-sinc affair in which each pursued the other possessively, obsessively, while being shamelessly unfaithful. By the end, when this dreary, often violent relationship between two selfish people had run its course, she loved him enough to shoot him, but not to let him go.

25

Then why has the story of Ruth Ellis continued to fascinate people? Why does the name of this part-time prostitute and night-club hostess win immediate recognition thirty-five years after her body was doused in quicklime and buried in the yard at Holloway prison?

There are many answers. In 1955, the murder took the lid off the new sleazy postwar London of after-hours drinking clubs, underworld figures and sex for sale. Ruth Ellis, who consciously modelled herself on blonde sirens of the screen such as Lana Turner and Marilyn Monroe, had resorted, too, to a Hollywood solution to her problems – a six-shooter. From a British standpoint, it was also the eternal class struggle expressed in sexual terms – blonde tart chases refined upper-middle-class, ex-public school boy.

But, if there was one reason people would never forget Ruth Ellis, it was because of the sentence pronounced on her at the Old Bailey. The execution of a woman who, at worst, should have been convicted of manslaughter, and who met her fate with such dignity, caused such a wave of disgust that the Ruth Ellis case played a significant role in Britain's abolishing the noose for good, ten years later.

And even today, the Ellis case retains its relevance as a classic example of male injustice meted out to a woman: a court now, hearing that gently bred David Blakely had punched the pregnant Ellis in the stomach, causing a miscarriage less than two weeks before the shooting, would likely free her, to the cheers of the public gallery.

For a young woman with a lot of verve and ambition,

Ruth led a messy life. Born Ruth Neilson, on October 9, 1927, in Rhyl, a North Wales seaside resort, she was the daughter of an unsuccessful musician who finally found work as a chauffeur and moved his family to London in 1941 in the midst of the Blitz. Ruth, the rebellious one of the four children, left school at age fourteen and took a series of dead-end jobs, including waitressing and minding a machine in an Oxo meat-extract factory.

Wartime London teemed with allied soldiers, and it wasn't long before Ruth was bringing home Clare, a French-Canadian service-man whom the family liked and she adored. His pay, more generous than that of British troops, introduced her to a life of meals out and taxicabs home, and she began to think about how life would be as his wife in Canada after the war. When she became pregnant just before Christmas, 1943, Clare said it was no problem: they would get married right away. Ruth's mother cannily wrote to his commanding officer. That was when they discovered Clare had a wife and three children back in Canada.

Ruth had learned a hard lesson about trust. She cried for days, then got a job as a cashier, where she could sit down. On September 15, 1944, she gave birth to a son, Clare Andria, who during his short and tragic life would be known as Andy.

Her entrance into the glamorous world of London's West End came with an advertisement offering a pound (about five dollars) an hour for models willing to pose nude for members of a London camera club. Some members, it was said, had no film in their cameras. She'd go for a drink afterwards, and that was how she met Morrie Conley, who ran several after-hours clubs and who would later be identified in the press as a major vice boss.

Ruth was flattered when Conley spent the whole evening talking to her, and even more impressed when he offered her a job as club hostess, a job paying five pounds a week plus 10 per cent commission on drink and food sales, and free evening dresses. Soon she was taking home twenty pounds a week, many times what she had earned doing drudgery in factories and restaurants. There was even more money to be made going to bed with the black marketeers and out-of-town businessmen who frequented the clubs.

When she met George Ellis, a Surrey dental surgeon, at the club, it seemed to Ruth she was finally ready to make that big jump to a fancy house and expensive lifestyle in the suburbs. Ellis, forty-one, was recently divorced, and couldn't get enough of Ruth. Marriage? Why not! Their 1950 marriage was a disaster. Ellis, who would eventually hang himself with his own pyjama cord in a hotel room, was an alcoholic. He beat her up several times, and, in 1952, expecting a baby, she left him and sued for divorce. With Andy and the new baby, Georgina, to look after, she turned to Conley again, and was soon back in the money, earning on one occasion a £400 tip from a satisfied customer with whom she had been on vacation.

One night she met a snot-nosed public-school brat named David Blakely who, typically, was getting his kicks from insulting the hostesses, Ruth included. She didn't give him another thought until Conley promoted her to manager of The Little Club, one of his joints in Knightsbridge. Who should the first customer be but the brat Blakely. This time she saw the other side of his character, and found him charming and amusing. Within a week he was sharing her bed in the little two-room flat over the club that was one of the perks that came with her new job.

Ruth's sex life in those days was devilishly complicated. In the afternoon, there were clients to be accommodated; Morrie Conley continued to make demands; and Desmond Cussen, a new man in her life, an ex-bomber pilot who Ruth used as a doormat and a convenience, was also on the agenda. The remaining two years of Ruth's life would be spent trying to make a living while keeping the various men in her life apart, occasionally satisfied and minimally disgruntled. Mostly she didn't succeed.

Blakely, three years younger than Ruth, was consumed by a passion for racing cars. The son of a Scottish doctor, he had developed this interest from Humphrey Cook, a former racing driver whom his mother married after her divorce. Never very successful at the track, Blakely nevertheless introduced Ruth to the champagne-and-engine-oil glamour of the weekend circuits. His dream was to manufacture 'The Emperor,' a sports car he and his friend, Ant Findlater, were developing. David, a former Guards officer who was supposed to be a hotel-management trainee, received an allowance from his stepfather, but with his flashy lifestyle and the money the sports car swallowed, he was always hard up and begging Ruth for money. A friend afterwards described him as 'a dead unreliable bastard.'

Ruth became pregnant by him in 1954 and claimed afterwards that David, who was engaged at the time to the daughter of a wealthy manufacturer, offered to marry her. 'I was not really in love with him at the time,' she said. She got an abortion one weekend when he was out of town. David's engagement ended soon after.

Adding to the tensions was the fact that David was ashamed to introduce Ruth to his family. One evening he drove her to Penn, in Buckinghamshire, where his mother and stepfather lived, but when he found his mother was in the pub, he refused to take her in, bringing a drink out to her in the car instead.

Before David Blakely came on the scene, Ruth had been proud of the job she was doing in making The Little Club hospitable and profitable, and was always looking for ways to improve it. Now, David would frequently arrive drunk, make a scene over the presence of Desmond Cussen and take her up to the flat, whence the sound of blows was clearly audible to the customers. Often, she said after, she was covered with bruises. When, in June 1954, David went to the Le Mans racetrack in France to drive and didn't return when promised, an angry Ruth took Desmond as her lover. These two men in her life, she would say, 'hated each other.'

By December, the club receipts were way down, and Conley fired her. With Andy, who was ten, coming home from boarding school for the holidays, she had nowhere to live. David was furious when he discovered that she had moved with Andy into Desmond's large apartment.

Almost immediately, she began sneaking out to spend nights with David at a hotel.

It couldn't go on, of course. Each of the men was bitterly jealous of the other. In February, Ruth made her choice: she left Desmond Cussen, and she and David rented a Kensington bedsitter in the name of Mr. and Mrs. Ellis. It was a pathetic comedown for the girl who, not long before, had been earning big money, taking elocution lessons and aiming for a career in the movies. And then things got worse. The Emperor, on which David and Ant had been pinning their money and their hopes, blew up in a race. 'It's all your fault,' a bitterly disappointed David told her. 'You jinxed me.' And then Ruth discovered she was pregnant again. At her trial Ruth would say: 'He did thump me in the tummy.' What she meant was that he first choked her, then punched her in the stomach, causing her to lose the baby.

It would be unfair to put the blame all on one side. On one occasion, following one of their violent encounters, friends noticed David's back was amass of bruises, and he admitted that Ruth had gone after him with a carving knife. She was drinking heavily and was subject to fits of extraordinary jealousy, especially in relation to David's friendship with Ant Findlater and his wife, Carole. Ruth knew that, some years before, David had had an affair with Carole. Now, whenever he was with the Findlaters, even though he often had to consult Ant about their car project, she interpreted it as an act of betrayal.

By now, they were so hard up she sometimes didn't eat all day, and Desmond Cussen was helping with the rent. David was talking again about them getting married, but he was becoming increasingly reluctant about returning every night to the depressing bedsitter, where young Andy, during the school holidays, slept on a camp bed alongside their double bed and where the rows rarely stopped.

'I'm supposed to be calling for Ruth at eight tonight,' he told the Findlaters at the start of the Easter weekend as they drank at the Magdala, 'but I can't stand it any longer. I want to get away from her.' Why didn't he leave her, asked Carole. 'It's not as easy as all that,' he replied. 'You don't know her, you don't know what she's capable of.' Carole suggested that David should stay the weekend with them.

At Egerton Gardens, the countdown to murder had begun. David was supposed to pick Ruth up at 7:30 p.m. By 9:30, he still wasn't there, and she phoned the Findlaters. Ant, who answered, denied David was there. Ruth called the one man she could rely on totally, Desmond Cussen, and asked him to drive her to Hampstead. Outside the Findlaters' Tanza Road flat, she saw David's station wagon. She rang the bell repeatedly, but there was no answer. When she phoned, the receiver was put down.

Deliberately, with icy fury, she took Desmond's flashlight and smashed in the rear windows of David's car. The police, who arrived shortly afterwards, took the lenient view and advised her to go home.

In the early hours of the morning, Ruth finally returned to Egerton Gardens. Instead of sleeping, she sat smoking all night. 'If only I had been able to speak to him and give vent to my feelings,' she would write later, 'I do not think any of this would have happened.'

Next morning, the pattern repeated itself. She rang Tanza Road, but the receiver was put down. After lunch she gave Andy money to go to the zoo and got Desmond to drive her to Hampstead again. Somehow she got it into her head that David was having an affair with the Findlaters' nanny. That evening, Saturday, there was a party at the Findlaters', and Ruth stood below, listening to the laughter, some of it she was sure David's as he chatted up a new woman. Around ten o'clock she saw him emerge with his around a woman she assumed was the nanny.

Throughout Easter Sunday, Ruth later claimed, she stayed home drinking Pernod. At 7:30 she put Andy to bed. The idea had formed in her mind, she said, of killing David. At Tanza Road, not seeing the station wagon, she walked the short distance to the Magdala, assuming David might be there. He had arrived a few minutes earlier on an errand to get Carole some cigarettes and to buy beer.

Did he recognize her as she walked down the sidewalk toward him? Was he trying to ignore her and get into the car quickly before she arrived? By then, even if he had greeted and spoken to her, it was probably too late. Ruth Ellis, as she opened her purse, had only one idea in her head.

Afterwards she would write, 'All I remember is the blood. I have never seen so much blood.'

In Holloway Prison for women, as she awaited trial, Ruth Ellis, who a jury member would afterwards describe as a 'common little West End tart,' turned out to be a lady after all. 'Please try to believe me when I say how deeply sorry I am to have caused you this unpleasantness,' she wrote to David's mother, as if she was apologizing for a gaff at a tea party. When Melford Stevenson, her chief barrister, pressed her for details that might help her case, she told him, 'Look, stop minding about me. I'm so sorry for you. It's such an awkward case isn't it?'

To the frustration even of the prosecution, she would make no effort to save herself. 'She was almost ludicrously offhand in her own defence,' Jean Southworth, who assisted the prosecuting barrister, Christmas Humphreys, has said, 'as if she didn't care.' It was as though Ruth, who had modelled herself on those tough broads up on the movie screen, was determined to play her last scene as if the cameras were rolling. She would show them that, like Lana Turner, like Gloria Grahame, she could spit in the teeth of fate. No apologies, no excuses, no cringing – that would be her credo. She'd play the role she'd written for herself to the last fadeout.

The one favour she asked of Stevenson was that he get permission from the prison governor to have her hair, which was darkening at the roots, returned to its pristine shade of platinum blonde for her appearance in Number One Court at the Old Bailey. And, vindictive to the last, her main concern about the trial was that the Findlaters should be exposed as the people who turned David against her.

The trial was a scandal. It was the shortest murder

trial on record, lasting just over one day. Ruth went into the witness box and told her story in that carefully modulated tone she'd learned at elocution classes and without ever betraying any emotion. Nothing was made of Ruth's 'thump me in the tummy' remark, and any defence was effectively destroyed when Christmas Humphreys got to his feet and asked her a single question: 'Mrs. Ellis, when you fired the revolver at close range into the body of David Blakely, what did you intend to do?' She replied: 'It is obvious when I shot him I intended to kill him.'

The jury took only fourteen minutes to find her guilty, and only a few minutes later she was on her way back to Holloway and the death cell. 'She wanted to die,' her older sister, Muriel, has said. She refused to appeal, and, said Muriel, 'Ruth had no patience with the people around her who were hoping to get her sentence commuted.'

The one question that had not been addressed at the trial was where Ruth had got the gun. She had told police an implausible story about acquiring it several years before from a club customer as security for a loan, and keeping it in her clothing drawer all those years. But the gun was properly oiled and showed no signs of neglect, and, for someone who had never handled a gun before, Ruth had seemed surprisingly competent in the way she used it. The day before her execution she finally told her parents and one of her solicitors, Victor Mishcon, that Desmond Cussen had given her the gun, shown her how to fire it and driven her to Hampstead the night of the shooting. Another of her lawyers said

Desmond admitted as much to him only two days after the killing. Desmond, who lives now in Australia, has denied the allegations in a television interview.

But even if Cussen's complicity had been revealed at the time, it would likely not have affected the outcome. The particularly dimwitted Home Secretary of that era, Major Gwilym Lloyd George (the cabinet minister responsible for reviewing the case), said later in defending his decision not to intervene, 'We cannot have people shooting off firearms in the street. As long as I was Home Secretary I was determined to ensure that people could use the streets without fear of a bullet.' Giving further support to this specious argument, the banker's wife who had been struck in the thumb by a stray bullet, Gladys Kensington Yule, wrote to a newspaper, 'If Ruth Ellis is reprieved, we may have other vindictive and jealous young women shooting their boyfriends in public.'

In prison, Ruth's icy disregard for her own fate disintegrated and, at one point, she threw herself on the bed in her cell, crying hysterically, 'I don't want to die. I don't want to die.' She asked her mother to smuggle a bottle of sleeping pills into prison for her. But, as the July 13 execution date approached, she regained her composure. 'Have you heard the big news?' she asked a friend visiting her. 'I'm not going to be reprieved. Don't worry, it's like having a tooth out.'

But there were others who did not accept her fate with such equanimity. Petitions were signed urging a reprieve, one by 50,000 people, and the largely dormant campaign against capital punishment sprang back into life. The morning Ruth was to die, Cassandra, the passionately abolitionist *Daily Mirror* columnist, wrote a column that would remain forever linked to Ruth Ellis in the memory of many. It began: 'It's a fine day for hay-making. A fine day for fishing. A fine day for lolling in the sunshine. And if you feel that way – and I mourn to say that millions of you do – it's a fine day for a hanging.'

Shortly before nine o'clock, Ruth was given a tot of brandy and drained the glass. Outside the prison a crowd of more than 1,000 waited, some of them chanting anti-hanging slogans. She was led the few feet to the execution shed where the final obscene rite was performed by Albert Pierrepoint, the state hangman. The executioner wrote Ruth's sister a letter afterwards, saying she had gone to her death braver than most men.

A few years later, when changes were being made at Holloway, the body of Ruth Ellis, or what remained of it, was released to her family, and she was buried in a country graveyard at Amersham, Buckinghamshire – far from the lights of the West End. There was a gravestone, but her son, Andy, had it removed to discourage curiosity-seekers. Andy, who led a disturbed life, committed suicide and is now buried with his mother. Her daughter, Georgina, born just as she was divorcing the child's dental-surgeon father, was brought up by a well-to-do Cheshire couple and didn't realize who her mother was until she came across a pile of clippings in a drawer one day, she told an interviewer in 1983. At the time, Georgy, as she's known, had four children, had chosen a modelling career and was living with her third husband.

In 1957, largely as a result of the Ruth Ellis case, the

37

concept of diminished responsibility was introduced into British law; had it been in force when she shot David Blakely, Ruth Ellis would almost certainly have gotten off.

That would have given no satisfaction to that section of the British public that went in fear of young women running rampage in the streets with revolvers. And neither, in a sense, would it have satisfied Ruth Ellis who, apart from those times when she experienced an only too understandable terror at what was about to take place, felt that natural justice was served by her execution. As she had written in a letter to David's mother: 'I shall die loving your son. And you should feel content that you have been repaid. Goodbye.'

She could not have conceived how, even forgetting the inspiration her story has provided for screen writers and authors ever since, the grim circumstances of her death have continued to reverberate in the lives of her contemporaries. After visiting the Magdala Tavern on a spring day exactly thirty-five years after the shooting, I had, by coincidence, to meet Brian Lane, an author, at the British Museum. Lane is the founder of The Murder Club, which publishes regional guides to historic murders in Britain. Before that, Lane informed me when I told him where I had just been, he was an ardent abolitionist whose desire to end the death penalty had been sparked by the hanging of Ruth Ellis, which had occurred when he was only fourteen. It's hard now to realize the shock that went through Britain when that happened, he said. And for him and for many other young people who had grown up in the shadow of the Second World War and in a world still governed by the old leaders and old values, it was the first awakening to the fact that everything wasn't black and white, that justice wasn't simply a matter of an eye for an eye.

A VERY
FINE LADY

Ruth Ellis couldn't spell, left school at fourteen and lived
what most would regard as a disreputable life; Jean Harris
was well-brought-up, highly educated and was the
headmistress of a posh private girls' school. What they
had in common was that, inspired by searing jealousy,
they both took up guns and shot down the men they loved.

It wasn't supposed to be that way for women like Jean
Harris. She was the new woman exemplified, the
professional, the unflappable powerhouse headmistress
of Madeira School for girls in McLean, Virginia, used
to giving orders, a strict enforcer of the moral code for
her girls. But beneath the veneer, she was a type familiar
throughout the history of female homicide, the woman
scorned. And her lover of fourteen years, the Scarsdale
Diet doctor, Herman Tarnower, her beloved 'Hi' was also
a type common enough in these dramas – the incorrigible
philanderer. For a while, in the aftermath of that night
when she forgot her gentle breeding and pumped four
slugs from her Harrington and Richardson .32 into
Tarnower, Jean Harris became a new sort of hero, a

feminist avenger. When the world learned that, behind the charm and popularity, Tarnower was a compulsive womanizer who played off his mistresses against one another, Harris initially engaged the sympathy of many women who, though liberated, still felt they weren't getting a fair deal in the bedroom.

Then what went wrong? And why is Jean Harris today serving out the last years of a fifteen-year jail sentence in the Bedford Hills Correctional Facility when everything seemed so right? She had the right story – that on the night of March 10, 1980, she drove from Virginia to Tarnower's home in Westchester, not to kill him, but to commit suicide beside a favourite pond in the grounds of the house where daffodils bloomed. She had the right lawyer, a brilliant but until then obscure counsel named Joel Aurnou, who showed a masterly grasp of the public-relations savvy so necessary to the modern trial lawyer. She had the right jury – it included eight women. And she had a judge so sympathetic that, while sentencing her, he declared emotionally, 'I wish personally, as you do, that the events of March 10 had never taken place . . . the best of luck to you.'

The only actor who didn't fit the script was Jean Harris, who thought herself too clever by far to learn her lines and who was let down in the final count by feelings and emotions no lady would admit to.

Harris, the stylish Wasp divorcée from Grosse Pointe, Michigan, met Tarnower, the upwardly mobile Brooklyn-born son of East European Jewish parents, at a dinner party in New York in 1966. Their first date they went dancing at The Pierre, although his manservant, Henri van der Vreken, came to pick him up and take him home sharp at 11:00 p.m. The following year Tarnower gave her a very large diamond ring and asked her to marry him, but soon got cold feet. The fact that Tarnower was still a bachelor at fifty-six, and had had a string of mistresses, frequently simultaneously, did not register as a danger signal with Harris.

On the face of it, their long-standing relationship was enlightened. They provided enormous intellectual stimulation for each other and travelled together to some of the most exotic spots in the world, from Khartoum to Afghanistan; she pretended not to notice his constant round of affairs with other women. Meanwhile, her own career as an educator had been advancing and, in 1977, she was appointed headmistress at Madeira, the unanimous choice of the board, she was assured. Board members might not have been as impressed if they had known of her affair with Tarnower − even the modern headmistress is expected to be celibate, decently married or, at worst, discreetly lesbian − but Tarnower lived a five-hour drive away in the expensive suburb of Purchase, in Westchester County, so there was little risk of exposure. Tarnower's own career took a dramatic twist when, in 1978, he was persuaded to turn the diet list he had been handing out to patients for twenty years into a book, *The Complete Scarsdale Medical Diet*, which became a huge best-seller.

Fame, money, success, with a side-order of sex: Harris and Tarnower seemed to have it all. However, appearances were deceptive. All through those apparently carefree years, Tarnower was also sharing his bed with

43

his nurse-receptionist, Lynne Tryforos, attractive in a feline sort of way and twenty years younger than Harris. Tryforos would send letters and personal messages to the doctor while he and Harris were globetrotting, and at New Year's, 1980, while the doctor was with Harris in Florida, Tryforos declared her feelings for him in an ad on the bottom of the front page of the *New York Times*: 'Happy New Year, Hi T. Love always, Lynne.' During the same festive season, Harris had presented Tarnower with a poem she had written, a spoof of 'The Night Before Christmas,' in which, barely hiding her hurt, she'd listed some of his girlfriends. 'In the guest room lay Herman, who, trying to sleep, was counting the broads in his life — 'stead of sheep,' it began.

Harris could accept the 'broads.' What she couldn't accept was that, slowly but steadily, Tryforos was displacing her, and Tarnower was making it clear that he wanted to sever his connection with the Madeira headmistress. To Harris it was insufferable. It was she who had helped Tarnower with the book, helped make him a 'star.' Now it was only fair that she should share in his glory, attending dinner parties and receptions with top-drawer people in Westchester. Yet, with an important testimonial dinner coming up for Tarnower on April 19, given by the Westchester Heart Association, he was proposing to take Tryforos instead of her. And Harris was losing her grip at Madeira too. An outside study had proposed her removal from the top job. She'd gotten a reprieve, but she knew her days there were numbered. In that final week, too, she had expelled four seniors after marijuana was discovered on school premises, a controversial decision that some felt was excessively punitive.

This, then, was the troubled Jean Harris who, on March 10, wrote her will, in effect resigned from her job and, after filling up the tank of the school's Chrysler, set out on a very rainy late-afternoon on the five-hour drive to Westchester. What was in her mind as the tires hissed, headlights blinded her, and, hour after hour, the miles dragged by? Suicide, she says. Murder, the prosecution alleged. Probably even she wasn't sure by the time of the trial.

As Harris battled through the rain that evening, Tarnower was arriving home from work at his sprawling home in Purchase. He was tense, having received a phone call from Harris at his office that afternoon, to say she was going to drive over for a talk. Well, that couldn't be helped. For now, he concentrated on the role he loved above all others, that of gracious host. Lynne and another woman friend were coming by for an intimate dinner, served by the obsequious Henri and cooked by his wife, Suzanne. It had been a tiring day; by 8:30 his guests took their leave and Tarnower, a habitual early-retirer, was in bed by 9:00. If Tarnower remembered Harris's promise to come and see him, he dismissed it, thinking she had probably changed her mind.

By 11:00, the only light on in the house was in Suzanne's room, where she was watching television. In his tower bedroom, reached only by an awkward spiral staircase, Tarnower was deeply asleep. We have only Harris' version of what happened next. Suddenly the bedside light was switched on. The doctor stirred, rubbed his eyes.

45

'Hi, I thought you would leave a lamp in the window.'

Then Tarnower was awake and sitting up. Harris must have come in through the garage door, which was always left open. She was sitting on the edge of his bed, rather foolishly clutching a bunch of daisies.

'Jesus,' he groaned, 'it's the middle of the night.'

'It's not really that late,' she said, 'and I'm not going to stay long.' He turned on his side and shut his eyes. 'I brought you some flowers.'

'Jesus, Jean,' he said, getting angry now, 'shut up and go to bed.'

His eyes were still shut. He was aware of her going into her bathroom. Then there was the sound of breaking glass. She had found negligées and a box of curlers belonging to Lynne Tryforos. She was tearing the place up. According to Harris, as she came out of the bathroom he slapped her across the mouth with his open hand. She threw another box at a cosmetic mirror, and he struck her again. Then, she went over and sat on what, in that house, was called, euphemistically, 'the guest bed.' When he turned again, Jean Harris was clutching a revolver, which she had just removed from her purse.

What happened next will never be known. We have only Harris's word for it. She says she intended to kill herself, but that, as she raised the gun to her head, Tarnower lunged across the bed to grab it from her. As they wrestled for the gun, it went off, sending a bullet through his hand. 'Jesus Christ, look what you did!' he screamed. As he headed for the bathroom, Harris claims she went down on her hands and knees to recover the gun, which had fallen to the floor. Once again, as she went to shoot herself, Tarnower 'flew over the bottom of the bed,' lunged for the gun and made her drop it. Bleeding profusely, Tarnower reached for the intercom buzzer on the phone to alert the van der Vrekens. As he picked up the phone, Harris again grabbed for the gun. As they wrestled for the weapon, Harris would say, she felt it go off and believed the bullet had struck her. 'My God,' was her supposed reaction, 'that didn't hurt at all. I should have done it long ago.'

But it was Tarnower who was crumpled on the floor between the beds. Harris claimed she tried to shoot herself once again before going downstairs and out into the night, looking for a pay phone to summon help. As a suicide attempt, it was ludicrous. The score: Tarnower four bullets, Harris none. There was a lot, in fact, that seemed odd in Harris's story. Why use the gun, purchased eighteen months earlier, when she had a medicine cabinet full of tranquillizers and stimulants prescribed for her by Tarnower that would have done a better job? And if suicide was the intention, doing it in the comfort of one's own home seems a pleasanter alternative than driving five hours in order to sit in the pouring rain beside a pond before pulling the trigger.

Suzanne van der Vreken, surprised to hear the buzzer go at night, had picked up the phone, heard screams, the sound of a struggle, Harris's voice, and then a gun going off. She'd called the police. Harris, seeing the first cruiser heading toward the house, had turned her car around and followed it back. Patrolman Danny O'Sullivan, a young officer who was one of the first on the scene, would later testify that Harris had told him she had driven from

47

Virginia to have Tarnower kill her. Oddly, this version was not denied by Harris or her defence team until four months later. O'Sullivan also said that Harris told him in those first minutes that Tarnower had slept with every woman he could, and she had 'had it.'

From the start, the public — and even the police — saw Jean Harris as a different sort of defendant. At the police station she was even allowed to wash her blood-spattered blouse — a shocking instance of tampering with evidence. And within hours, Joel Aurnou, a former Westchester judge, had been engaged in her defence and she had been released on $40,000 bail. From that point until her trial, which began in White Plains, N.Y., on November 21, 1980, the version put out by the defence team, and apparently accepted by the media and the public, was that Jean Harris had been tormented beyond reason by the obsessively promiscuous Tarnower. The suggestion that Tarnower, who was sixty-nine, was throwing over the able and highly educated Harris, fifty-seven, for a younger woman of lowlier status evoked a certain sympathy with many women who shared her aspirations. The defence might be that Harris intended only suicide, but there was a vicarious feeling that justice after all had been done.

Aurnou's whole strategy in the trial — a mistaken one, as it turned out — was to present Harris as 'a very fine lady, of the kind you don't see much any more.' Indeed, Harris, in her tasteful suits, blouses and sweaters, something different every day, looked the part, while a stream of witnesses from her school — board members, teachers and students, all impeccable — would make the trial seem sometimes like a testimonial dinner for some revered 'Mrs. Chips.'

But the picture didn't quite add up. The van der Vrekens, who had witnessed Harris's degradation at close hand throughout the years, were not sympathetic, but visibly hostile toward her in the witness box. Such an 'immoral murder,' Henri called it.

In her asides to journalists covering the trial, Harris sounded, well, glib. 'He's a genius,' she said of her lawyer. 'He may get me off.' Get her off. But wasn't she supposed to be innocent? The arrangements at the Tarnower house – where Tryforos's and Harris's clothes each had to be concealed to prevent the other's discovering them and where, following a Caribbean trip with the doctor, Harris found some of her clothing ripped and slashed – seemed so . . . *unseemly* is the only word. Not surprisingly, Harris took an active part in her defence, constantly briefing Aurnou, telling reporters she wasn't satisfied with the way 'the truth' was being concealed, snapping once at a junior member of the defence team who tried to muzzle her, 'Shut up! If you say that again, I'll . . .'

Central to the question of whether Harris had struggled with Tarnower for the gun and shot him accidentally or whether she had simply shot him down was the evidence of the forensic experts, and here the jury had to choose whom to believe. Dr. Louis Rou, deputy medical examiner for Westchester County, maintained that the doctor's wounds were not consistent with a struggle having taken place. But Herbert MacDonnell, a crime-scene expert who had testified in the Robert Kennedy and Martin Luther King assassinations, produced elaborate calculations to

49

show that bullet trajectories confirmed Mrs. Harris's story of what had happened.

In the end, just as Aurnou had known all along, it came down to the impression Harris made on the jury, and when he called her to the witness box he was confident that what the jury would see was a refined and sensitive person of intelligence and good sense, inherently incapable of killing another. It must be said that Harris, by any normal standard, was an excellent witness – generally calm, eloquent, if sometimes rather wordy in her answers, and occasionally moved to tears. But early on, she showed an inclination to be testy with the young prosecutor, George Bolen. 'No,' she replied when Bolen asked her if a card inscribed 'Love, Hi,' which came to Harris with a gift of roses, was dated. 'I think you've already discovered, [in her responses to earlier questions] Mr. Bolen, I don't put dates on things.'

Aurnou wanted the jury to see Harris as the vulnerable woman who, facing failure in her career and rejection from her lover, had written in her last note to the college administration, 'I was a person and no one ever knew.' What had she meant by that? her lawyer asked softly. 'Jean, look at me.' Finally she responded in a voice close to breaking: 'I don't know. I think it had something to do with being a woman who had worked a long time and done the things a man does to support a family (she had two grown children) . . . but I wasn't sure who I was, and it didn't seem to matter.'

Aurnou: 'It mattered to you, didn't it?'

'I was a person sitting in an empty chair, Joel, I can't describe it any more.' (The jurors must have wondered

50

sometimes if they were in a courtroom or eavesdropping in a psychiatrist's office.) Jean Harris, prompted by her counsel, was touching the right chords, evoking themes instantly recognizable to millions of women treading the lonely pathways of power.

There was an almost dreamlike quality to her description of the actual shooting – no talk of blood and screams and anger, but, instead, a sort of frozen ballet of misunderstandings, abrupt and inappropriate gestures, ending, incongruously, with Tarnower collapsed between the two beds. As she'd stroked his face afterwards, she had said, 'Oh, Hi, why didn't you kill me?' In no sense, though, had she come to Purchase with the intention of having Tarnower shoot her, she claimed. As a person who had spent his life saving others' lives, he wouldn't have done it. All she had wanted, she said, was 'a quiet, pleasant last few minutes.'

But if the words suggested vulnerability, Harris's aggressive attitude in the witness box was sending the jury a different message. At one point, as Bolen questioned her, Harris turned to Judge Russell Leggett: 'How long do we go on this way, Mr. Leggett? This is not what I understood we were going to do.' Ignoring her gross impertinence, the judge reminded her that she had a lawyer to make objection on her behalf. 'He's not saying a word,' she snapped. 'Oh, come on, Bolen,' she remonstrated a few moments later, 'you are throwing something into this that's silly.' Her replies to him were withering, as if she were dealing with a particularly dense college junior requiring a reprimand.

Diana Trilling, in her excellent study of the Tarnower

murder, *Mrs. Harris*, has argued that Aurnou was so overwhelmed by his client, was so impressed with her abilities and so blind to her flaws that he didn't see the unfortunate effect her overbearing personality had on others. If he hadn't been, perhaps he would have used psychiatric evidence to put forward an insanity defence. Because Aurnou should have realized there was one crucial piece of evidence that could, in an instant, destroy the image he had tried to create of a civilized and sensitive woman inherently incapable of murder.

On the day of the murder, Harris had written Tarnower what would be called the 'Scarsdale letter,' a very lengthy, very detailed account of her grievances. The defence team had retrieved the registered letter from the post office before it was delivered, and a prolonged legal battle ensued over whether the prosecution could demand to see the letter. Although Bolen had won that skirmish, neither Aurnou nor Harris seemed to realize the impact the letter would have. Once Bolen, in his flat voice, stumbling occasionally, read the letter in court, the jury saw Harris in a new light.

The immediate reason for writing the letter is the April 19 testimonial dinner to which Tarnower was proposing to take Tryforos instead of Harris, and which she describes as the apex of his career. Harris tells Tarnower in the letter that she has told a mutual friend she would be there, 'even if the slut comes – indeed, I don't care if she pops naked out of a cake with her tits frosted with chocolate.' Harris can't find words harsh enough to describe her rival: 'vicious, adulterous psychotic,' in one place, 'your psychotic whore' in another.

52

She taunts Tarnower with his 'fourteen years of broken promises.' Examples: 'I want to buy you a whole new wardrobe, darling. Let me buy you an apartment in New York, darling.' She complains: 'I have watched you grow rich in the years we have been together, and I have watched me go through moments when I was almost destitute.' Money is a constant note in the letter, the nickels it cost her to phone him, the expense of travelling to Westchester to see him, the money she admits she took from his wallet to pay for damage done to her clothes at the Purchase house while they were away on a trip. Incredibly, toward the end she says, 'You have been what you carefully set out to be, Hi − the most important thing in my life . . . and that will never change.'

At one level, it is a love letter; however, it is also a shriek of pain. But, for the jury, what had to be startling, disconcerting, was the depth of rage that prompted the ladylike Jean Harris to use such violent language about her rival. And perhaps for the first time they could see that the woman in the box, the woman who could look at her lover's bloodied pyjamas in court with imperturbable calm, the woman not above putting the judge in his place, might be capable of anything.

The one person missing from this trial, which ran for three months, was, as is usually the case in a murder trial, the victim. Jean Harris had completely dominated these proceedings, and the jury heard little about Dr. Herman Tarnower, and that nearly all bad. In the last moments, just before the final speeches, they were allowed a snapshot of him. On the stand, Harris had described her last phone call to the doctor on the morning of March

53

10, when she had asked him not to read the letter when he received it, and, she insisted, they had talked amicably about who should be invited to dinner when she visited him on April 5. But Juanita Edwards, a longtime patient of Dr. Tarnower who was in his examination room when that call came in and overheard the doctor's end of the conversation, recalled it differently when she was called as a rebuttal witness. She heard Tarnower say, 'Goddammit, Jean, I want you to stop bothering me.' Then: 'You've lied and you've cheated.' The doctor, she said, was tense when he resumed the examination.

The jury took eight days to decide, and with each day that went by, the defence team became glummer, interpreting delay as an indication that the jurors were hardening themselves for a guilty verdict. Their premonition was correct. Harris was found guilty of second-degree murder and two incidental weapons charges, and on March 20, just over a year after Tarnower's death, looking wan and, for once, unkempt, Harris appeared for sentencing. Summoning those reserves of strength that had always surprised those watching the trial, she told Judge Leggett with a final flash of arrogance: 'For you and Mr. Bolen to arrange my life so that I will be in a cage for the rest of it, and that every time I walk outside I will have iron around my wrists, is not justice; it is a travesty of justice.' She was, she insisted, innocent of the crime.

Her supporters cheered her statement and Judge Leggett, forgetting, perhaps, that a jury of her peers had found Jean Harris guilty of the deliberate shooting down of a fellow human being, was almost apologetic as he gave

54

her the mandatory sentence of from fifteen years to life, with no possibility of parole for fifteen years. 'Mrs. Harris, I found you to be a brilliant, brilliant woman,' he said, and added that he was urging the prison authorities to allow her to make use of her gifts to help improve the lives of other women prisoners.

Jean Harris has responded to that challenge. Her appeal failed, as have her requests for clemency. But, despite suffering a heart attack in 1984, she has written two books about conditions in women's prisons and helped start a children's centre where inmates can play with their children during visits. She will become eligible for parole in 1996, when she is seventy-two.

MOM'S
THE WORD

Jean Harris dominated a Westchester courtroom in 1980 by the sheer force of her personality — and lost; eighty-five years earlier a black tailoress, a woman of equally strong character, held a Toronto courtroom in her thrall — and with a very different result. The case began with a riddle. The murder of young Frank Westwood confounded the authorities for the longest time, and Sir Arthur Conan Doyle, the creator of Sherlock Holmes, consulted by a Toronto newspaper, pronounced the case 'a strange and absorbing mystery.' It was, indeed, that. Beyond the question of who killed young Westwood, what intrigues us today is the light the case throws on race relations at the end of the last century, the odd business of cross-dressing in Victorian times and, above all, the puzzling character of Clara Ford, one of the most unusual women ever to face a murder charge in a North American courtroom.

October 6, 1894, was an unusually mild evening in the city of Toronto, and brought out groups of young people who stood joking and laughing under the streetlights of Jameson Avenue in the city's west end. Several of them noticed Frank, the eighteen-year-old son of Benjamin Westwood, a well-to-do fishing-tackle manufacturer, making his way home around 10:25 p.m. At the foot of the street, he opened the gate and walked up the path to Lakeside Hall, his parents' home, which the newspapers would describe as 'palatial' but which was, in fact, simply a comfortable Victorian mansion in a choice position overlooking Lake Ontario.

His father had already gone to bed, but his mother, whose favourite he was, was still reading in the dining room with the blinds open. He joined her there and they sat talking for ten minutes or so, and then Frank put out the gaslight and they went up to bed. He was on the second-floor landing when he heard the front doorbell jangle. It was the maid's night off, so, shouting to his mother that he would get it, Frank ran back down the stairs, relit the gaslight in the hall and went to open the door.

A few moments later his mother heard a loud crash and a shattering of glass. She heard her son cry, 'Mother, Mother, I'm shot!' Mrs. Westwood screamed, then called to her husband, 'Ben, bring your revolver. There's a burglar in the house.'

Dashing downstairs in his pyjamas, Westwood, Sr., found his wife bending over Frank, who was lying on the floor in the hallway. He tried to get by her, but she stopped him. 'Don't go out there. They might try to shoot you,' she said. He ran back up to his room, pulled on his pants – who would dare shoot a man once he had his pants on! – and grabbed his Bulldog revolver from the desk in his bedroom. Rushing out to the front steps, Westwood fired a shot in the air. The sound of the gun echoed back from the lake at the foot of the garden. There was no one there. No one, in fact, would report seeing young Westwood's attacker arrive or leave.

Doctors were summoned, the police arrived, and the boy, still alive, was carried up to his bedroom where he was able to tell officers that all he could see of his assailant was that he was wearing dark clothing and had a slouch hat pulled down over his face, but that he had a moustache.

Next day, as Frank's condition worsened, journalists combed young Westwood's past in search of a motive. The worst anyone would say of him was that he had once been seen skinny-dipping in the lake with his friends, and that he smoked more cigarettes than his father thought good for him. Two days after the shooting, with his life ebbing away, Frank gave what, in those days, was called, starkly, 'an ante-mortem statement' to the county crown attorney. In it, Frank stuck to the earlier description he had given of his attacker, and said he had never seen him before. No, he replied to one question, the man was not Gus Clark, a disreputable character whom Frank, a short while earlier, had caught breaking into a building on the waterfront. All he would add to what he had said before was that he and his attacker 'fooled around in the hall for a few minutes' before he was shot. Then, beckoning the crown attorney to come closer, he said something rather odd: 'Mom's the word.' Was he joking? As the lawyer pressed him, he sighed, 'You can't pump me.' He

59

died shortly afterwards, and no fewer than four clergymen presided at his funeral at Mount Pleasant Cemetery.

The city was abuzz with gossip and theories. The classic scenario at that time would have involved Westwood getting some respectable young woman pregnant and her father having come gunning for him. But Frank simply didn't seem to have had any girlfriends.

Hector Charlesworth of *The World*, Toronto's best-known journalist, sent the details to Conan Doyle, who was lecturing in Chicago as part of a North American tour, and Doyle, then probably the most famous fiction writer in the world, promised to review them. But when he arrived in Toronto to give a talk at the King Edward Hotel, Doyle told Charlesworth he was as baffled as anyone. Although Doyle had, in fact, solved some real-life mysteries in the past, he insisted modestly that fiction was a lot easier than fact: one simply made up the clues to fit the solution one had in mind. Coming at it from the other direction was not as simple.

The inquest into Westwood's death dragged on for weeks, hearing evidence, it seemed, from everyone who had ever known him from the cradle on before the jury arrived at a verdict that death was caused 'by the hand of an unknown person.'

People had begun to forget about the shooting when, on November 20, some seven weeks after it had occurred, police, acting on a tip from the disreputable Gus Clark, arrested, not a man, but a mulatto or half-caste tailoress named Clara Ford and charged her with murder. Clark, a pickpocket, claimed that Clara Ford had admitted to him while they were drinking together that she had shot Westwood.

Evidence was not hard to find: in the room she rented on York Street, police found a suit of men's clothes that Clara admitted were hers and that she said had been left behind by another boarder. Even more damaging, they also found a .38 revolver, which, when fired into a side of beef, produced bullets with an identical nick on the side to that found on a bullet removed from Westwood's body.

The World reported: 'The girl gives her age as 33, but looks more like 25. She is best described as a 'yaller' girl and would almost pass for a white woman.' Born in Toronto, Clara had grown up in a small cottage at the back of the Westwood property, cared for by Mrs. McKay, a white washerwoman who had since died in the home for incurables. For the last two years, Clara had been living at Chloe Dorsay's restaurant and boarding house for coloureds at 152 York Street.

As to the motive for the murder, the editors of *The World*, taking a deep breath, prepared to introduce their gently-brought-up readers to evidence of human depravity beyond imagination. 'There is considerable reason for believing that this young woman is a sufferer from what the medical authorities call homo-sexuality, in other words that she was suffering from what is called sexual perversion,' the paper reported breathlessly. 'Such women go about in male clothing. They prefer masculine work and show an unusual skill in it. They eschew female occupations and often show a weakness for smoking and spirits. With this perverted condition there often go

61

pronounced outbreaks of passion and jealousy which drive the unfortunate victim to crime.'

A medical man, said *The World*, had stated that if young Westwood had interfered in any way with Clara Ford as she masqueraded as a man, threatening 'one of her dearest pleasures,' it would have been enough to provoke the fatal attack. Another characteristic of these creatures, the paper added darkly, 'is that they revel in blood.' This did not mean, *The World* hurried to assure its readers, that she was not a good tailoress.

But as Clara's story emerged, it became apparent there was another reason behind her wearing men's clothing. Some thirty-five years earlier, a young black woman had gone to work as a maid for a well-to-do Toronto family. She had become pregnant by the son of the house and, like right-thinking folk, they'd fired her. But a few days after the baby – Clara – was born, her mother had left her in a basket on the family's well-scrubbed doorstep. They had placed the child with the washerwoman, Mrs. McKay, giving her a sum of money that was soon spent. As she grew up, Clara was treated as if she were Mrs. McKay's own daughter, and was taken along from one grand house to another as Mrs. McKay made her laundry rounds.

When she was in her mid-twenties and after she had learned her trade as a tailoress, Clara struck out for Chicago, but found the only employment open to a black girl was hustling on Polk Street. No one ever faulted Clara Ford for lack of initiative: she bought some boys' clothing, a cap and some dungarees, tried a boyish swagger in front of the small spotted mirror in her rented room, slipped down the stairs when no one was around and emerged the complete urchin. Right away, the huskily built Clara landed a job as an hostler, caring for horses in a livery stable.

The work suited her, and Clara began to enjoy the advantages being a male gave her. Her voice was deep, and she was even asked to join the choir at the local Episcopalian church. She was taking confirmation classes there when, by cruel coincidence, a woman who knew her from Toronto recognized her and exposed her masquerade. Clara was sent on her way, but not before she told the minister she wanted nothing more to do with men. She may have had her reasons: during her time in Chicago, she was married, but her husband abandoned her after a year, leaving her with one child, maybe two.

After the build-up in the press, it was not surprising that the magistrate's court was packed the day after Clara's arrest, with citizens eager to see a living, breathing sexual pervert of the female gender. Among the crowd, though, were a fair number of members from Toronto's black population of 1,500 who came to show their support and to see that Clara got justice. Justice in her case might be swift: the police had already announced that Clara had confessed to the murder of Frank Westwood, so it seemed just a matter of formality before she was sentenced to hang.

As the prisoner was led in, heads craned eagerly. What they saw was a dejected-looking figure wearing a beaver-trimmed cloth coat and a feather-trimmed fedora over her short, curly hair. Her strong features were masked by a yellowish pallor, as if she hadn't slept, and her eyes were downcast. How did she plead? Her 'Guilty' was barely audible. Then something seemed to click inside Clara Ford's head. She looked the magistrate straight in the eye, squared her shoulders and said in a voice that could be heard right to the back of the room: 'Not guilty!'

Clara would languish in the Don Jail for five months, reading books sent to her by well-wishers, before she was brought to trial on April 30, 1895, before Mr. Chancellor Boyd. Her supporters had put the intervening months to good use, raising funds to hire as her lawyer E.F.B. Johnston, the Canadian Clarence Darrow of his day, a counsel who, in the British tradition, would communicate with his clients only through a subordinate, never talking to them face to face — except when they were in the witness box.

After the details of Westwood's death were gone through once again, the prosecution turned to proving that Clara Ford had a motive for the killing, and aroused only hilarity in the courtroom. Mrs. Libby Black swore solely that, one night, Clara had come up to her in the street and told her with regard to Westwood, 'If you speak to him again I will do for you.' Mrs. Black did not appear a likely object of jealousy, and under questioning she admitted she was serving a thirty-day sentence for drunkenness. Asked to describe the clean-shaven Westwood, she said he had a moustache, and yes, she finally admitted, the police had told her they would help her get an early release if she testified against Clara. Laughter followed Libby Black from the witness box.

In Detective-Sergeant Harry Reburn, a police veteran of twenty-two years, the prosecution was much more confident it had the ammunition to convict. At four o'clock on the afternoon of November 20, Reburn testified, Clara had been brought to his office, and he had cautioned her. Did she know why she was there? About the Frank Westwood murder, she replied, but she had not shot him. She couldn't have done, she claimed, because she was at the Toronto Opera House that evening seeing a play, *The Black Crook*. Who with? With Flora McKay, a fourteen-year-old black girl who had also been brought up by Mrs. McKay and who lived on Richmond Street.

Oh? said Reburn mildly. Well, it would not take long at all to bring Flora to the station to confirm Clara's story. A short time later, the frightened Flora was ushered in. Yes, she whimpered, she had arranged to go to the theatre that night with Clara. And, had they gone, asked the stern sergeant. She had waited half an hour, admitted Flora, and Clara had not turned up. Reburn then said that a friend of Clara's, Mrs. Crozier, was willing to say that, when Clara left her home about nine o'clock that night, she was carrying a revolver stuffed in her waistband.

Reburn testified that he was turned away, lighting the gas, when Clara said, 'There's no good misleading you any longer.'

'Are you going to make a statement?' he asked. 'It will be heard in evidence against you.'

'I don't care. I deserve it.'

'What do you mean?'

'I shot Frank Westwood.'

'What for?'

'Because he attempted once to take improper liberties with me, and I told him I would get even with him.'

The language has the wooden inauthenticity of the policeman's notebook, but Reburn said Clara told him that, after leaving Mrs. Crozier's that night, she had slipped out of her skirt and hidden that and her other female clothing under the wooden sidewalk at a deserted spot at the foot of Dufferin Street, then walked from there to Jameson Avenue, a journey taking about fifty minutes. She had waited in the shadows outside Lakeside Hall until she had seen Frank Westwood go into the house. When the downstairs lights were put out, she had gone to the door and rung the bell. She had fired only one bullet, the sergeant quoted her as saying, and she had meant only to scare him – not to kill him. Afterwards, said the sergeant, Clara had reclaimed her clothes, changed, and returned home along the waterfront.' Why, asked the defence counsel, had Reburn testified at the preliminary hearing that Clara had returned by the water in front of the New Fort (better known in this century as the Stanley Barracks)?

'It's not right,' said Reburn, flustered. 'It's taken down wrong.' Could he have changed his evidence, Johnston wondered, because of an article in the *Toronto Telegram* in which a reporter described how he had tried to follow the route as Reburn had described it and had found the water too deep in front of the New Fort for anyone to pass? Reburn admitted he had discussed the article with his superior, Inspector Stark, and they had gone to the New Fort and were unable to get by it because of the depth of the water.

Flora McKay, bringing a bright spot of colour to the drab courtroom with her red tam o'shanter, agreed that Clara had failed to keep their date to go to the theatre and added that, when she saw Clara a week later, 'she told me if the missis (of the house in which Flora was now working in domestic service) asked me where I was, to tell her we were at the theatre together.' The prisoner in the dock closed her eyes.

In fact, said Mrs. Crozier, filling in the picture, when she had come to her house that night, Clara had said she was supposed to be going with Flora to the theatre, but when she saw it was nine o'clock she said it was too late. As Clara was leaving, one of Mrs. Crozier's daughters, Maggie, had lifted back Clara's coat and said, 'Oh, Clara has a revolver!' Clara always carried a gun, added Mrs. Crozier.

This fact was confirmed by Benjamin Vise, a top-hatted Jewish tailor for whom Clara had once worked and who noticed the gun one day when her coat had fallen to the floor. She told him she carried it for her protection. Vise then recalled another conversation he had with Clara.

'I suppose you will see me married one day,' she had told him.

'To whom?' he had asked.

'Gus Clark.'

'Gus Clark!' said Vise in surprise. 'Will Gus Clark marry a coloured girl?'

'He takes me buggy riding every night,' she replied. 'If he doesn't, I'll do him up the way I did a man in the States.'

'I got scared,' said Vise. 'I fired her right away.'

67

It seemed as though, one by one, the doors were slamming shut for Clara Ford. William Elliott, a foreman gunsmith, confirmed that, when he had fed bullets from her gun into a side of beef covered with two shirts and a vest to simulate a human body, he had found marks on the bullets identical to those on the bullet removed from the body of Frank Westwood. The marks were caused by an irregularity in the barrel of the rusty and inferior weapon, he said. Yes, he admitted under cross-examination, the gun was a cheap model and there were thousands of them in use. And yes, he had seen others with the identical flaw in the barrel.

The ballistics evidence had been, to some extent, undermined, but as the prosecution's case concluded, Johnston and his client faced discouraging odds. Clara's signed confession had been admitted as evidence and even those close to her, Flora and Mrs. Crozier and her daughters, had testified against her, one daughter remembering that, on the night of the murder, Clara had been wearing men's trousers beneath her skirt. Johnston was able to produce the manager and an usher from the Toronto Opera House who claimed to remember seeing Clara, a regular customer, at the theatre that night. But their evidence carried little weight against the word of Flora, who appeared to have no reason to lie. The defence lawyer put character witnesses, including the minister at Clara's church, on the stand to attest to her industry and honesty. But, in the end, the desperate and, in those days, highly unusual practice of having the accused enter the witness box seemed her only hope.

Not for nothing had Clara Ford spent many of her

evenings off in the thirty-five-cent balcony seats at the theatre. If she fancied herself an actress, this was the moment when her very life depended on her delivering a brilliant performance. She went into the box boldly, concealing any feelings of nervousness, and faced Johnston with her head high. The signed confession? A sham, she declared, extracted from her by relentless police bullying, which went on from 4:00 p.m., when she was taken to Reburn's office, until 11:40 p.m., when she finally signed the statement.

The sergeant, she said, had started out telling her, 'Clara, if you don't tell the truth, it will be the worse for you.' Then, she said, he had tried to wheedle around her, sitting close to her and saying, 'If you was my own sister, I couldn't think more of you. Only say that he insulted you. He's dead now and can't say anything.' And then, leaning in confidentially and winking: 'There's five hundred or six hundred dollars offered in this case. I'll see you are a freed woman and walk the street yet.' Was the policeman suggesting she would receive the reward for her own capture? Clara didn't explain.

For three hours she kept the packed courtroom enthraled, her voice sinking to a whisper as she described some of the details of her life, and then rising in anger when she was asked about the evidence against her. The statements of Flora and Mrs. Crozier given at the police station? 'Why, they was half scared to death,' she said, rolling her eyes and mimicking the fear and trembling of the two witnesses.

At one point, she said, Inspector Stark had come into Reburn's office and, after asking her questions about her style of dress, had told her it was illegal for a woman to go about in men's clothing. Then how was it, she snapped, that Vic Steinberg, a woman journalist with *The Globe*, (a Toronto newspaper), wore men's clothing to baseball games? (Clara was not to know, but, earlier in the century, Dr. James Bridie, a military surgeon who practised in Canada, was found upon his death to have been a woman. And, at other times, both Greta Garbo and one of the historic characters she played in movies, Queen Christina, wore men's clothes to escape their gender. 'I long to escape my destiny,' the queen had once exclaimed.)

Some would say that Clara's performance that long afternoon, sometimes standing defiantly with her hands on her hips, other times laughing out loud at the allegations against her, was a little over the top. And when the prosecutor, Hartley Dewart, rose from his seat, his first question was: 'You are a woman of good intelligence?'

'I am,' she replied.

'And not easily rattled?'

She scented the trap: 'I was badgered and confused.'

In his summing up, Johnston moved quickly to capitalize on the strong impression Clara had left with the jury. 'Would you wonder, with such inhuman, such brutal treatment as she was subjected to by the police, that a woman would say anything to get away from the clutches of these vultures? This woman,' he said, speaking metaphorically, 'was taken by the throat and the statement choked out of her by a man who was merciless, relentless. I am almost ashamed to think I am a man when

70

I realize that a fellow-citizen of mine could be guilty of
conduct of that kind.' The courage of the prisoner in
taking her life in her hands and entering the witness box,
he said, 'was the boldest, the noblest, the most heroic act
ever witnessed in a criminal trial in this city. Think,' he
said, ending on a note of bathos, 'of this poor Negro girl.'

The judge remained unmoved. The jury, he said, should
exercise caution in the case of a woman going into the
box, knowing her life was at stake. He reminded them
of the words of Job in the Bible: 'Skin for skin, yea, all
that a man hath will he give for his life.' The jury was
all-white and, in an age when women jurors were unheard
of, all-male. But Toronto, priding itself still for the role
it had played earlier in the century as a haven for slaves
escaping from the South, took a certain satisfaction in
its sense of fair play toward, if not complete tolerance
of, blacks, and, in fact, had just elected its first black
alderman to city council. When they retired, the members
of the jury found themselves split nine to three in favour
of acquittal. Forty-eight minutes later, they returned with
a unanimous verdict: not guilty.

As happened so often when a woman was acquitted,
cheers rang through the courtroom. Over the noise, Clara
made a little speech, thanking the jury for their verdict,
and then invited them all to Chloe Dorsay's for supper.
In the street, a huge throng formed behind Clara and her
friends as they walked back to the restaurant where Chloe
was still fulminating over an incident during the trial.
When she had gone into the box to testify that Clara had
returned home by eleven o'clock on the night of the
murder, and had mentioned reading about the Westwood

71

case in the paper the next day, the judge had asked her to read a passage to prove she was literate. She didn't have her reading glasses with her, she had to admit. They could be sent for, said the judge, anticipating some fun at Chloe's expense. When Chloe's glasses were brought to her, she read a portion from the newspaper with no difficulty at all. 'Just imagine!' she said, still trembling with indignation, 'Me, who lived here when this town was called Muddy York and there were no sidewalks or streetcar tracks! Me, who taught school here for eight years!'

Clara had already received an offer to appear in a Toronto dime museum wearing her suit of men's clothes and acting out the murder. 'I don't approve of that,' said Chloe firmly. 'It's un-Christianlike and not in keeping with the scriptures.' Against the scriptures or not, Clara could not resist, and she was soon giving theatrical performances, in which, laughing at the law, she re-enacted the shooting of Frank Westwood.

It was too much for Johnston, her lawyer, who felt he was being made a fool of. Breaking his usual rule about talking to clients, he sent for Clara, suggested that performing in a dime museum was totally unseemly, and advised her to leave town. Surprisingly, Clara did as she was told, encouraged no doubt by financial considerations, and we next hear of her appearing in the American West with Sam T. Jack's Creoles and billed as 'the woman who killed a man in the name of the unwritten law.' That law, of course, allowed a woman to use any force necessary to repel an attack on her virtue.

Did Clara kill young Westwood? I think there is little

doubt that she did. Her motive? The police said she told them that, one night, Westwood had grabbed her and tried to take liberties with her. Why didn't she stop him? 'Well, you know my colour. I would have had no chance against a man like that in his position,' she replied. Growing up on Jameson Avenue, she said, she had always been the butt of abuse and name-calling. The shooting, she implied, was her way of getting back at those who had abused her.

We can sympathize with Clara, but can we really accept that explanation? I don't think so. She was thirty-three, of strong build, and she had, by her own admission, knocked around the world some. It's hard to imagine her being intimidated by the clumsy advances of an eighteen-year-old. Another possible explanation is that old wild card, love. If she and Westwood had been having an affair and the boy had made her promises he wasn't prepared to keep, perhaps Clara, after a lifetime of insults, had decided to take the law into her own hands.

Another intriguing possibility, suggested to me by a correspondent, is that Clara, in shooting Westwood, was acting, not as a spurned mistress, but as an avenging mother. We have to look at the ages here to get the picture. Clara was not of Westwood's generation. Flora, on the other hand, at fourteen, was much closer in age to the young man. There were strong rumours at the time that Flora was Clara's natural daughter. Asked in court how long she had known Flora, Clara replied, 'As long as I can remember.' And Flora's complexion, lighter even than Clara's, suggests the father might have been a white man.

If so, then a pattern emerges: Clara's mother had been seduced and cast aside by a white; Clara, too, may have had the same experience. If Frank Westwood had seduced young Flora, could it have been that Clara, unwilling to see the same pattern repeated in the third generation, had gone after him with a gun? It's an interesting theory that at least goes partway to explaining why Clara shot a man little more than half her age.

As for Lakeside Hall, like Clara, it's been lost sight of. In the 1950s its gables and peaks and Victorian conceits disappeared beneath a highway, the Gardiner Expressway.

MURDER AT
THE SAVOY

P.D. James has said that a body on the drawing-room floor is more horrible and, indeed, more interesting than a dozen bullet-ridden corpses down Raymond Chandler's mean city streets. What engages our interest, she suggests, is the 'contrast between order, normality, hierarchy and the dreadful and contaminating option of violent death.'

Ms. James might have had in mind the shooting of Prince Ali Kemal Fahmy Bey, which occurred one sweltering summer's night in 1923 in the Savoy Hotel, in London, the British Empire's high temple of order and decorum at that point in history. And for a heroine of the story, even Ms. James could not have imagined anyone more fascinating than Madame Fahmy, a French woman who was every bit as impressive in the witness box as Clara Ford, and who, before this was over, had won a nation's hearty approval for her act of homicide.

The suite where it happened, one of the hotel's most elegant, overlooking the River Thames, is still very much as it was then, although when I visited it I found no musty reminders of past misdeeds. Instead, as the door swung open, I was met by the springtime fragrance of an English cottage garden.

The source was immediately obvious: in the entrance to this suite, where many of the world's wealthiest people and some of the biggest names in show business have stayed, stood a vast bunch of spring flowers, delicate narcissi dancing between tulips big as teacups.

Another large bouquet, this one of pink roses, was framed by the tall windows of this honey-panelled drawing room, and beyond was the panorama of the River Thames – coal-black barges, busy tugboats and, above, a watercolour grey sky. From these windows that night in 1923, the view must have been truly. stupendous. Following days of sweltering heat, London was experiencing the most frightening thunderstorm of a generation. Black thunderheads rolled down the river from the direction of Kingston, thunderclaps set the windows shaking, and again and again the sky was split by daggers of blue lightning.

But between the peals of thunder, John Beattie, a porter, wheeling a cart of luggage down the plush-carpeted hall at 2:30 in the morning, heard the unmistakable sound of three gunshots. Dashing back down the corridor and coming around the corner, he came upon Prince Ali Kemal Fahmy Bey, slim, handsome, immensely rich at twenty-two, dying of gunshot wounds outside the door of his suite. Standing over him, in a shimmering white, low-cut evening dress, now splattered with blood, and holding a Browning .25 automatic pistol, was his French wife, Marguerite Fahmy.

'What have I done!' she cried repeatedly in French

before throwing the gun down beside her expiring husband. And then, falling to her knees, implored him, 'Speak to me, speak to me.'

Only moments before, Beattie had come across Fahmy in the hallway outside his door, clearly in a state of agitation. 'Look at my face! Look what she has done!' he told the startled porter, pointing to a faint pink mark on his cheek. At that point, his wife had come out of the suite and started to berate her husband in French, pointing to her eyes. Beattie, as best he could, had urged them to be quiet and return to their suite before they wakened other guests. He had trundled his wagon only a few steps down the hall when he heard a whistle and, looking around, saw Prince Fahmy trying to coax their small dog back through the open door, into the suite.

If the murder had occurred in working-class Whitechapel, just across the river, it would have been written off as a 'domestic' and dismissed in a few lines in the following day's newspapers. But this was a high-society murder with exotic foreign overtones. Better still, as the case unfolded, there were delicious hints of sexual depravity, and, if that wasn't enough, the British public found in Madame Fahmy a touching and attractive heroine, a woman the newspapers would call 'The Tragic Princess.'

Sir Edward Marshall Hall, one of England's most famous legal counsels, would capitalize on this natural sympathy to conduct a defence, which, by the lights of that day was considered brilliant but which, by modern standards, has to be counted the nastiest piece of racist demagoguery ever to disgrace a British courtroom. It

77

prompted a protest from the Egyptian government of the day, although little satisfaction was gained. That's not to say that Prince Fahmy was an endearing character. He was a spoiled playboy who treated women with violence and contempt. But it's hard to avoid the conclusion that his wife had long intended to murder him and was only waiting for a suitable chance.

Prince Fahmy inherited something like five million dollars – an unimaginable sum in those days – when his father, an Egyptian cotton magnate, died while the boy was still at school. The youngest of four children, with a Caucasian mother and three older sisters, Ali (who, in letters to friends, signed himself with the nickname boys at his English public school had given him, 'Baba') had been spoiled rotten at home. After his mother died when he was seventeen, he was free to run wild, and was soon in the hands of blackmailers. Wiser heads in the family prevailed, rescuing him from embarrassment, persuading him to set aside sizable chunks of his income for the education of the poor, and employing Said Enani, an official working with the Egyptian ministry of the interior, to be his secretary-keeper.

Marriage, his relations thought, might settle Ali down, but he was not interested in any of the demure and well-connected young women of Cairo whom they had in mind. He was looking for someone more exotic, and at a reception in Cairo, in January 1922, he met a French woman of obvious style and charm who was visiting the Egyptian capital at that time. Marguerite Alibert, the woman he would marry, claimed afterwards that he had immediately offered to put on a Venetian fête for her, but that she had coldly turned him down before leaving a day or two later for Paris.

If she intended to catch him, she could not have baited the hook more compellingly. By July, when she was staying at her house by the sea in Deauville, Ali was in Paris, and this time his methods were subtler. In Deauville, Marguerite found herself befriended by a woman from Morocco; after they returned to Paris, the woman phoned to say there was a man Marguerite simply must meet. Intrigued, she agreed to accompany her friend for tea at the Majestic Hotel, and found herself looking into Prince Ali's expressive brown eyes.

As they left together for the fashionable Château Madrid restaurant, Ali tried to impress her with a piece of princely showing-off. Which car would she care to travel in, he asked with an airy wave at the two automobiles parked at the curb, the Rolls-Royce coupe or the sporty open Torpedo? Marguerite was not easily impressed. She let him know in short order that she owned her own lavish apartment on the Avenue Henri Martin, had her own car and employed two maids and a chauffeur.

It's easy to understand why Ali was infatuated with her, showered her with jewellery, and even bought her a car she obviously did not need. Marguerite, tiny, with huge dark eyes, represented to Ali the sophistication of Paris, and the fact that she was divorced and ten years older than him made her only that much more intriguing.

By the time she returned to Deauville in mid-August, Ali was making what she would call '*des avances furieuses.*' Rejected once again, he got his secretary,

79

Enani, a neat little man who wore Western suits, to plead his case, singing Marguerite the old alluring song of Ali's immense fortune. She did finally agree to have Ali accompany her to Biarritz in September, not, she claimed, because of the diamonds from Cartier's or the bracelet of coral and emeralds he lavished on her, but simply because she liked his smile, 'which was like that of a child.'

They dined in the best restaurants and went on excursions to Spain, but still Marguerite refused to commit herself, and he left for Italy, from where he bombarded her with passionate letters. When he got home to Cairo, he declared in a letter that she was 'the torch of my life,' and said his only thoughts were for 'your bewitching charm, your exquisite delicacy, the beauty of your heart.' He signed his letters 'your faithful little Baba.' She succumbed and agreed to meet him in Egypt only when he announced he had fallen ill. 'I am dying,' he declared. 'Your name alone is on my lips.'

When she arrived in Alexandria on November 22, the Ali who came bounding aboard the ship to meet her showed no signs of ill-health. She, in turn, showed no surprise. In Cairo, he installed her in his palace, the interior a copy of Fontainebleau, her room designed specially for an earlier guest, the King of Serbia. There were so many gold cigarette cases lying around, she would write later, 'that they got in the way.' Her safety was assured by the presence of twelve black servants in uniforms bearing Ali's stylized monogram — servants she would shortly view as her jailers.

For now, however, Marguerite felt as if she had

wandered into the Arabian Nights. Her charm overcame the objections of Ali's sisters, and finally she agreed to marry him – but not without proper caution. She made a stipulation in the marriage contract that, although she would wear the black veil of a Moslem bride for the ceremony, there would be no purdah for this daughter of the Champs-Elysées, and she got Ali's agreement that, contrary to the usual Moslem custom, she would have the right to divorce him if the marriage did not work out.

On December 26, the civil ceremony took place. But, in the course of the religious ceremony that followed, Marguerite discovered that Ali had pulled a fast one and that she would not, after all, be granted the right to seek a divorce. As the guests waited uncomfortably on their antique gilt chairs, the bride and groom and their respective advisers went into lengthy negotiations, and, after four hours, the deal was set. Marguerite would give up her right to divorce in return for a lavish gift and Ali's promise of undying fidelity. For her, it turned out to be a poor bargain.

Perhaps it was the note of acrimony that crept into the pre-nuptial negotiations, or maybe it was just the unconventional sexual demands Ali put on his bride, but surely a honeymoon was never so shortlived. After a banquet at Shepherd's Hotel, the couple boarded Ali's yacht, which had a crew of twenty-five, for a honeymoon cruise up the Nile to Luxor where world attention was focusing on the discovery on November 4 by Lord Carnarvon of the burial chamber and treasure of King Tutankhamen.

But Marguerite was making her own discoveries. No

neophyte in sexual matters, she was shocked when she found that Ali's interest in her was confined to acts of sodomy. It was a blow to her self-esteem. She, the sought-after darling of the Paris salons, realized her husband saw her as no more desirable than the pretty youths he bantered with, and whose significance now became apparent.

Almost immediately, Marguerite and Ali were having furious arguments in public and slapping each other's face. After one row, Ali forbade her to go ashore and left his uniformed guards to see she didn't escape.

It would not be long before photographs of Marguerite wearing the latest fashions would be emblazoned on front pages all over Europe and North America as the central figure in a notorious murder trial, but Ali had his own ideas about taking her picture. In the Valley of the Kings, he got her to climb into an ancient sarcophagus, close her eyes and cross her hands, in the style, perhaps, of the dead Cleopatra. The theme of entombment depicted in the photograph may have been more than symbolic: a few days later, Marguerite sent a document to her lawyer in Paris, which, she instructed him, should be opened only in the case of her death or disappearance. In it, she declares: 'I, Marie Marguerite Alibert, of full age, of sound mind and body, formally accuse in the case of my death by violence Ali Fahmy Bey of having contributed to my disappearance.' The day before, January 21, 1923, he had sworn on the Koran to kill her, she claimed. The reason, she would explain later, was that she refused to return to him some of the jewellery he had given her earlier.

82

Around the same time, Ali, displaying his spiteful sense of humour, was writing to Marguerite's sister with whom, inexplicably, he had struck up a chummy correspondence: 'Ha, ha, ha, just now I am engaged in taming her. Yesterday, to begin, I did not come in to lunch or dinner, and I also left her at the theatre. This will teach her, I hope, to respect my wishes. With women one must act with energy and be severe.' His 'energy' included punching his wife and dislocating her jaw when she returned from a solitary visit to the cinema.

However cynical Marguerite's reasons for marrying Ali may have been, she now faced a terrifying future. Subjected to violence by her husband, watched over by a new Algerian bodyguard she called the 'Black Hercules' and far from her friends, she was little more than a prisoner. And then, unexpectedly, the door of her prison opened. Ali, without telling his wife, had accepted a diplomatic post with the Egyptian embassy in Paris. Even up to the time they boarded ship for Marseilles, he gave her no hint of their destination, and on board the conflict continued, with Ali at one point locking her in her cabin for twenty-four hours.

But once they were back in her beloved Paris, even with the bodyguard lurking nearby, Marguerite was free to see her friends again, to go riding and to attend the theatre. Now here is the surprising thing: considering the treatment she had received and the death threat she claimed her husband had made against her, the most natural thing in the world would have been for Marguerite Fahmy to leave her husband and sue for divorce. It's hard to believe she did not, in fact, consult her lawyer and, discovering

83

the difficulties in the way of getting a divorce and a decent settlement, turn her mind to alternative ways out of her predicament.

On July 1, Prince Ali Fahmy Bey, exhausted with the diplomatic round in Paris, travelled with his wife and an entourage that included a valet, two maids and the ever-present Said Enani to London where he proposed to holiday at the Savoy Hotel. For Marguerite, the journey must have been an uncomfortable one because first thing she did on arrival at the hotel was to have the front desk summon Dr. Edward Gordon, who had his office across The Strand, to examine her for a painful and particularly unglamorous complaint, haemorrhoids, a condition she believed was connected to her husband's sexual demands.

Dr. Gordon, not one to neglect a wealthy patient, visited her daily for the next eight days, prescribing medications and finally bringing in a specialist, who on the morning of July 9 − Ali Fahmy's last full day alive − suggested she enter his nursing home for an operation.

It was to be a day full of tensions, mysteries and flare-ups. Some time that morning Marguerite received an anonymous note in French warning her not to return to Egypt because she would be poisoned or otherwise killed there in what would be made to appear an accident. 'Remain in Paris with those who love you and will protect you,' the note concluded.

At lunch, Ali and Marguerite argued furiously over the proposed operation. Enani would say later that Marguerite wanted to return to Paris to have the procedure performed, while her husband wanted her to enter an English nursing home, as the specialist had suggested. Was Enani being entirely frank? In a note Marguerite wrote to Dr. Gordon after lunch, but for some reason did not send, she said, 'Doctor, things have come to a crisis. My husband refused to take the responsibility for my operation. I am therefore returning to my family – that is to say, tomorrow I leave for Paris.' She concluded: 'Will you please pay the specialist for his trouble? This account is a personal one.'

Against this tense background, on an airless and humid evening, Prince Ali prepared to enjoy what he had planned as one of the highlights of his London visit, a box at Daly's Theatre in Leicester Square to see *The Merry Widow*. We can only imagine the effort it took Ali, Marguerite and the inevitable Enani to maintain their smiles and civilized small talk as they gazed down at the lesser mortals in the pit.

But as soon as the couple returned to the Savoy, open hostilities were resumed. Marguerite twice refused to dance with her husband in the Savoy Grill and was heard to threaten to smash a bottle of champagne over his head. When the obsequious orchestra conductor asked Madame if there was a piece of music she would like to hear, she replied, in French, that she was simply not in the mood for music because 'my husband is going to kill me tonight.' With the tact for which the Savoy is famous, the conductor replied that he hoped to see Madame in the best of health tomorrow.

There is evidence that, as Marguerite went up to their fourth-floor suite, Ali was in a cab on his way to Soho. His purpose is unknown, but if he was in search of vice there was ample opportunity for it in that colourful

85

quarter of London. At any rate, he could not have dallied long because, when Beattie, the porter, saw him in the corridor at 2:30 a.m., he was wearing mauve silk pyjamas and backless green velvet slippers. Moments later his blood was staining the Savoy's broadloom, and according to the evidence from the autopsy, bullets from his wife's revolver, one of a matched pair they kept beside their bed for security, had smashed through his upraised arms before penetrating his skull.

Against a backdrop of lightning and thunder worthy of Wagnerian drama, Marguerite sobbed to Arthur Mariani, the night manager, who had hurried to the scene: 'I have been married six months and I have suffered terribly.' Dr. Gordon, always nearby when comforting was needed by the comfortably off, would say that Madame Fahmy, in her agitated state, had told him that her husband had threatened to smash her head in and, back at the suite, he had threatened her again and she had fired the pistol through the window to warn him off. Later, when he advanced on her again, she told the doctor, she had fired the gun at him, believing it was unloaded now and not realizing a fresh bullet would automatically drop into the firing chamber. When Ali slumped over, she thought he was shamming and lost her head and fired two more shots. Dr. Gordon noted that his patient had a scratch on the back of her neck that might have been made with a fingernail.

The trial of Madame Fahmy (she was not entitled to use the title 'princess') began at Number One Court at the Old Bailey on September 10 and attracted world-wide attention. The accused was represented by three of the

86

most expensive lawyers in England, led by the redoubtable Sir Edward Marshall Hall, while the Fahmy family interests were represented by several Egyptian lawyers. Women spectators, who made up a large part of the crowd in the public gallery, leaned forward eagerly as Madame Fahmy, a tiny figure in a black coat (the weather had long since turned cool) and a small cloche hat with a veil, was asked how she pleaded and replied in a low voice, '*Non coupable*' – not guilty.

The defence had spent money unstintingly in digging into the prince's background, and as Said Enani took the witness stand for the prosecution, two very elegant young Egyptians, supposedly intimates of Ali's brought specially from Cairo, sat prominently at the defence table. They never testified, but the unspoken message conveyed to Enani was that, if his testimony strayed too far from the facts, witnesses could be produced to correct the record. Even so, Enani's memory of threats Ali was supposed to have made against his wife proved spotty. He did admit that his employer frequently quarrelled with women and that Ali and Marguerite had come to blows. Marshall Hall's final remark to the witness, after producing a cartoon from an Egyptian satirical magazine showing Enani with his employer, was: 'I suggest that the association between yourself and Fahmy was notorious in Egypt!'

'That is not so,' replied the secretary coolly.

The crowds that queued up, sometimes from two in the morning, to gain admission were, of course, waiting to hear Madame Fahmy testify. On the day she was to take the stand, the prosecutor, Percival Clarke, with the

jury absent, asked permission of the judge to question
the accused woman about her past. 'I want to prove,' he
said, 'that she associated with men from an early age,
and that she is a woman of the world in the widest sense.
I submit that I am entitled to ask her how she treated
other men. I do not want it to be thought that all the fault
is on her husband's side.' The public gallery that day was
with Clarke to a man – or rather, a woman. But they
were to be disappointed: the judge, Mr. Justice Rigby
Swift, tersely refused permission for a prosecution fishing
trip, and Marguerite Fahmy, frail-looking and leaning on
a wardress, made her way to the witness box.

Testifying in French, her words translated by a young
woman barrister thoughtfully brought over from Paris
by the defence, she told the unhappy story of her brief
marriage, sobbing frequently. The last tragic night, she
testified, 'He said, "I will kill you," and crouched to
spring. I lifted my arm, so . . . I did not know how many
times the pistol went off. I did not know what had
happened. I saw him on the floor and knelt down beside
him. I caught hold of his hand and said, "Sweetheart,
it is nothing, speak to me!" ' At that point in her
testimony, Madame Fahmy broke into helpless weeping.

Under Clarke's aggressive questioning, though, she
showed no lack of mental adroitness. 'Can I correctly
describe you as a woman of the world?' he asked, getting
to his feet.

'I have had experience of it,' she replied carefully.

'Did you go to Egypt with the idea of living with him
or marrying him?'

The warm brown eyes looked suddenly helpless. 'I had

decided nothing. I loved him so very much and wished to be with him. I accepted to be his *amie*.'

Why hadn't she left her abusive husband when she had a chance in Paris?

'Where would I have gone?' she replied.

'You had a flat in Paris.'

'He would have fetched me back from there the minute he returned.'

'Haven't you many friends in Paris of influence and wealth?'

And then the clincher: 'I did not want my friends to know my sorrow,' she said softly.

Had she hated her husband? Dangerous ground here. Madame Fahmy paused, and then gave the absolutely correct answer: 'I did not hate him. I only hated the things he wanted me to do.'

With a master stroke, Marshall Hall waited until re-examination before introducing the explosive letter that Madame Fahmy had sent to her lawyer from Egypt regarding the death threat allegedly sworn by her husband on the Koran. Marshall Hall's technique right from his opening speech had, in effect, been to put Prince Ali on trial and thus divert attention from his client's possible failings. 'Fahmy Bey,' he had thundered at the start of the trial, 'shortly before he was shot, attacked his wife like a raving, lustful beast because she would not agree to an outrageous suggestion he made – a suggestion which would fill every decent-minded person with utter revulsion. Almost throughout their miserably tragic life of six months, this treacherous Egyptian beast pursued his wife with this unspeakable request, and because she

89

— immoral though she may have been — resisted him, he heaped cruelty and brutality on her until she was changed, by fear, from a charming attractive woman to a poor, quaking creature, hovering on the brink of nervous ruin.'

Strong stuff, but the great defender saved his worst vitriol for his summing up, which one writer has called 'the greatest defending speech of his life,' but which appealed in the baldest terms to the racial prejudices of the English jury.

Madame Fahmy, he said quietly, 'made one great mistake — possibly the greatest mistake any woman of the West can make. She married an oriental. I dare say,' he went on, 'the Egyptian civilization is one of the oldest and most wonderful in the world. I do not say that among the Egyptians there are not many magnificent and splendid men. But if you strip off the external civilization of the oriental, you have the real oriental underneath. And it is common knowledge that the oriental's treatment of women does not fit in with the way the Western woman considers she should be treated by her husband.'

Now Marshall Hall advanced on the jury box, inviting the jurors to picture that terrible thunderstorm the night of the murder. 'Imagine its effect on a woman of nervous temperament who had been living such a life as she had lived for the last six months — outraged, abused, beaten, degraded. In sheer desperation, as he crouched for the last time' — and Marshal Hall matched his words by crouching with the revolver in his hand — 'crouched like an animal, like an oriental, retired for the last time to get a bound forward, she turned the pistol and put it to his face. And, to her horror — the thing went off!' With these words, the lawyer, defying every consideration of safety, swung the gun until it pointed at the jury and then, for maximum impact, dropped it clattering to the floor.

He concluded his astonishing performance by reminding the jury, which included two women, of a popular novel of the time, *Bella Donna*, by Robert Hichens, in which the heroine marries a man of the desert. 'You will remember the final scene, where the woman goes out of the gates of the garden into the dark night of the desert.' At that moment a shaft of sunlight pierced the gloomy courtroom. Marshall Hall, not one to ignore a godsend, held his hand up as if bathing in the light. 'I ask you to open the gate and let this Western woman go back into the light of God's great Western sun,' he cried.

It was useless for Percival Clarke to point out that the heroine of *Bella Donna* had tried to murder her husband, useless for him to remind the jury that it was Madame Fahmy who was on trial, not her late husband. It took the jury only an hour to arrive at the verdict: not guilty. The cheering was so unrestrained the judge had to order the courtroom cleared of spectators before discharging the prisoner.

The verdict, of course, had little to do with the facts of the case. My feeling is that Marguerite Fahmy had decided some time before her husband's murder that she would never return to Egypt with him. Even if she succeeded in gaining a divorce in France, she was still far more likely to collect her winnings as a widow than she was as a divorcée.

91

The scenes in the Savoy Grill, the note to the doctor — handed to him when he attended her after the shooting — and the timing of the shooting with a porter conveniently near at hand to witness their last row, all suggest careful stage-managing. If Fahmy was about to spring on her, how was it that he was shot in the corridor and not in the suite? And is it likely that a man whistling for his dog would, no more than a minute later, become a ravening monster who must be shot down?

What was the evidence about Marguerite Fahmy's past that Percival Clarke was prevented from introducing? In a London newspaper 'morgue,' I came across galley proofs of an article entitled 'Life of Mme. Fahmy,' unpublished perhaps for libel reasons. Marguerite Alibert was the daughter of a cab driver and a laundress, the article said. Strikingly beautiful, she was by the age of sixteen already a cocotte, earning her living from men, and soon became the mistress of a department-store owner. He was the first of a series of lovers, many of them wealthy foreigners visiting Paris, who paid handsomely for her favours. She was married briefly to an Alsace businessman, Frederick Muller, and to another store owner named Laurent, and she had a daughter who, at the time of the trial, was attending boarding school in England. A young Mexican mining heir, a former Turkish ambassador with whom she lived in Cairo for three months and an Egyptian general, all figured in her life before she met Ali Bey.

Following her acquittal, Marguerite returned to her flat on the Avenue Henri Martin and she later starred in a movie in which she played the part of an Egyptian wife

– again wearing a Moslem wedding veil. Meanwhile her lawyers had commenced a lengthy battle in the Cairo courts over her widow's inheritance, which Fahmy's relatives were, understandably, contesting. At one point Marguerite was involved peripherally in a crooked scheme cooked up by a Cairo businessman whereby she was to fake a pregnancy and supposedly have the child, who would afterwards be reported as having died. Under Egyptian law her right to inherit would have been stronger if she could claim she had had a child by Fahmy.

In 1930, after a six-year court battle, Marguerite lost the last roll of the dice. The Cairo court ruled that, since she had shot her husband, she had no right to his fortune, which was then estimated at seven million dollars. It had all been for nothing.

LIZZIE, YOU'LL
KILL NO MORE

Lizzie Tilford reminds me of my Great Aunt Ruth from Seven Sisters in Wales. Like Lizzie, Aunt Ruth told fortunes and, like Lizzie, she was an unforgettable mixture of the sacred and the profane, a larger-than-life woman who, fifty years after her death, is still the talk of my relations in Wales. Aunt Ruth, they will tell you after the second sherry, would entertain the minister in her bedroom on Sunday afternoons – and get her husband, who was a bit simple, to bring them tea in bed afterwards. But, no one ever accused Aunt Ruth, as many did Lizzie, of giving her husband arsenic.

Lizzie married three times – one husband for love, she told people, one for spite and one for envy. She never did say which was which. By her account, she married her first husband, Fred Yates, in England when she was fifteen. 'I did it more for a dare than anything else. The girls bet me five shillings I would not dare marry him. We only lived together for a week or so, then we separated, and I never saw him again.'

Then, Lizzie would have us believe, she devoted her

life to good causes, becoming, in turn, a Girl Guide leader, a Sunday-school superintendent, secretary of a branch of the Comrades of the Great War, and a member of a choral society, topping off this record of selfless service by marrying a miner, William Walker, who was a Salvation Army sergeant-major, and becoming herself a Salvationist.

In 1928, the couple arrived in Canada with their four children, and Walker made a futile attempt at farming, before he fell ill, going blind and lingering for a few months before dying in Woodstock, in southwestern Ontario, on February 19, 1929. A brain tumour was listed as the cause of death.

Lizzie, ever resourceful, kept her family by working at a galoshes factory and telling fortunes. A steady stream of Woodstock women — and a few men too — found their way to her parlour to have their palms read or to learn the future from the bottom of their teacups. She saw no conflict between these activities and going to church, and it was at the Baptist church that Tyrrell Tilford, a thirty-one-year-old teamster, noticed her, a large, pleasant-looking woman, singing in the choir. When it came to showing a proper fervour, Lizzie, who claimed to be in her mid-forties at the time but was in her mid-fifties, did not believe in half-measures. Introduced to Tyrrell's elderly mother, she threw her two-hundred-pound bulk thunderously to her knees and began to pray aloud. Perhaps this was considered a teeny bit excessive; when she and Tyrrell were married on November 10, 1930, his relations stayed home.

Nevertheless, the Tilfords allowed Tyrrell to build for

him and Lizzie a small house at the corner of their lot on Cronyn Street (where it still stands, a cheerful clapboard-and-shutters affair), though relations between Lizzie and the old folks were never cordial.

Then, early on the morning of Friday, March 29, 1935, Tyrrell's seventy-four-year-old father, James, heard a scratching noise at the back door. He thought it might be an animal or a child. But when he opened the door, he found his son on his knees, trying to reach the latch. 'He came bundling in, all doubled up. He was as black as a chimney sweep,' Jim Tilford would later say. Helped to the couch, he gasped, 'I've come to tell you, Dad, I'm going to die.' He had to stop to catch his breath. 'I'm full of arsenic. Look at my tongue, Dad. It's all cut to ribbons.' Lizzie and her two grown sons, he claimed, had been dosing him with arsenic, putting it into everything he ate and drank, giving him capsules of the white powder and even pouring it on his tongue.

Tyrrell told his father he'd seen Bill Blake, a friend of his wife's who was always around their place ostensibly learning the fortune-telling business, peer at him from behind the curtain covering the bedroom doorway and heard him say, 'My God, he's had enough poison to kill twenty people!'

When his frail mother came downstairs, Tyrrell urged her to phone Keith's drug store to find out if arsenic had been sent to his home. 'Not for weeks and weeks' was the answer she got when she phoned.

'Mother, that's a lie, and a big one,' retorted Tyrrell when she told him what had been said. Dr. Hugh Lindsay, who had been treating Tyrrell, was called, but when he produced some capsules containing headache powders similar to those he had prescribed earlier, the patient said weakly, 'Them's different to what she (Lizzie)'s been making.'

When he called again the following morning, Dr. Lindsay told Tyrrell breezily, 'You look better already. You'll be up and about by Tuesday.'

'Why, you damned fool,' said the older Tilford, not one to mince words, 'he's dying now.' By Saturday night, indeed Tyrrell was feeling worse. 'I'm dying,' he told one of his brothers. 'You better fetch Lizzie.' When she arrived, Lizzie was all cooing concern. 'You know, honey,' she said, enveloping him in her arms, 'you should not have come up here.'

Tyrrell pushed her away: 'You've been poisoning me, Lizzie, and you know it. I'm going to die.' When she tried to soothe him and make light of his fears, his father butted in: 'You great cow, can't you see the lad's dying?'

'Honey, you're not going to die,' she said, ignoring the father.

'Yes, I am,' insisted Tyrrell. 'There's enough money in the insurance to bury me and then you can have your man with the two farms, Bill Blake.' Turning to his family, he said, 'When I'm dead, have my stomach analysed. They'll find arsenic. Lizzie, you've killed two, but you'll kill no more.'

Flushing with anger, his wife marched to the telephone, called Keith's drug store and demanded to know if arsenic had been sent to her house. She held out the receiver so that the hostile Tilford family could hear the reply and said, 'I want you to bear witness to that.'

Tyrrell, pale, panting for breath, and with a proper sense of drama, called his mother to his side. 'I want to give you a last kiss, Mother,' he said.

Not knowing what to do about their son's accusations, the old couple later went to bed, leaving Lizzie to watch over Tyrrell. Hearing a sound in the middle of the night, Jim got up and went to the kitchen. There was no sign of Tyrrell or Lizzie. On previous occasions Lizzie had been seen lifting her 155-pound husband and carrying him as if he was no more than a baby.

All the next day, the old people fretted, but did nothing. Early Monday morning, Tyrrell's mother thought she heard her boy shout. She hurried to the door, but outside everything was still. When she phoned his place across the yard, Lizzie reassured her, 'He had ice cream, a wing steak and apricots and a smoke yesterday – and he kept them all down.' Later that morning her sons told her that Tyrrell had died at five that morning – before she had spoken to Lizzie.

Dr. Lindsay, who had been away for the weekend, was in a quandary over what to put down as the cause of death. After consulting the coroner and the crown attorney, he listed influenza and a weak heart on the death certificate. Talk of poison at that time seemed only 'street rumour,' he would say later.

Lizzie was in a fever of anxiety that the Tilfords would call in the police. At the funeral home, she told a friend, 'I had him out of the coffin myself to make sure he was all right.' His organs, to her relief, had not been tampered with. 'I made sure he had his underwear on,' she added with a chuckle. 'I had my first husband (she probably

99

meant Walker, her second husband) out of the coffin too.'

Even with Tyrrell safely underground, she still worried. Unable to sleep one night, she sent one of her grown boys to the cemetery to make sure no one had dug him up. And when one of her late husband's brothers, Frank, came calling, she told him if his parents kept up their accusations, 'I'll sue them for every penny they've got. I'll make them print an apology in every newspaper in Canada.'

By now local gossip had it that strychnine and arsenic had been delivered to the Tilford house for killing rats, and Tom, another of Tyrrell's brothers, decided to find out once and for all if there had been a call for rat poison. 'By golly, Lizzie,' he said one day as he came in the door, 'you should do something about the rats around here. A twelve-inch one just jumped across my boot.'

'Oh, Tom, there are no rats here. Never have been,' she blurted out. And, she added, there wasn't any rat poison around the house either. Anyway, she said, seeking to reassure or maybe distract Tom, she would soon be talking to his dead brother again.

'How do you figure that?' he said, intrigued.

'Oh, I see. You don't believe in spiritualism,' she said.

The Tilfords got no response when they tried to get the police to investigate Tyrrell's death, so they finally took their suspicions to the provincial attorney general in Toronto. Only then, and by the light of lanterns in the middle of the night, did spades strike into the fresh earth of Tyrrell's grave. His dying wish was finally respected: his vital organs were removed for analysis, and his body was returned to the grave before daybreak. Professor

100

Joselyn Rogers, head of analytical chemistry at the University of Toronto and known to the public as 'the chemical detective' for his involvement in many criminal investigations, was able to report shortly afterwards that he had found two grains of arsenic in the stomach – enough to kill.

A month after Tyrrell's death, the Tilfords finally got the inquest they'd been demanding, and Victor King, a scrawny nineteen-year-old who worked as an assistant at Keith's drug store, went into the witness box, clutching the shop's poison book. He had delivered two ounces of arsenic to the Tilford home on March 20, he testified. Lizzie's sixteen-year-old daughter, Isabella, had signed for it, and there was her signature plain to see in the poison book.

Yes, agreed Isabella when it came her turn to testify, she had signed for the poison. 'I was alone in the house with my brother, William, when the poison came,' she said. 'Between two and two-thirty I telephoned Keith's drug store for the arsenic because Dad (Tyrrell) had asked me to do so. He wanted it to kill rats in the barn.' Where was her mother? 'At a birthday party. She left home about one-thirty,' replied the girl.

'You know Mr. King?'

'Yes.'

'You paid Mr. King?'

'Yes, two dimes. My father gave them to me out of his pocket.'

'What did you do with the parcel (of poison)?'

'Dad came in the back door and I gave it to him and he went over to the barn.'

'Did you tell your mother?'

'No. My father told me if I told Mother about it, it would be the worse for me.'

'When did your father commence to get sick?'

'The next day. Mother said to get Dr. Lindsay.'

'Did you ever know your father to vomit like that before?'

'Yes, on Valentine's Day when he ate too much ice cream.'

'What did your mother do when Mr. Tilford was ill?'

'She babied him up.'

'Did you ever tell your mother about this arsenic?'

'Yes, eleven days after father was buried.' At that point Isabella burst into tears and was excused.

Hutchinson Keith, the druggist, had a different version to tell. He had known Mrs. Tilford for several years, and she frequently phoned him for goods, he said. About 12:30 p.m. on March 20, she called him and said, 'Is that Mr. Keith? Can I get some arsenic? Since my husband has been collecting waste paper and garbage the whole place is overrun with rats.' Said Keith: 'She told me to send two ounces.' He knew it was Mrs. Tilford's voice. He recognized her English accent.

Victor King, recalled to the witness stand, said Mrs. Tilford called again later and asked him, 'When are you bringing out that parcel? I've got to go out.' King also remembered that a few days after Tilford's death, when he was making a non-toxic delivery to the house, Lizzie asked him, 'Aren't you kind of shaky?' 'No, why should I be?' he replied. 'Well, you brought some poison out here,' she said with a significant smile.

On June 11, with clumsy Speedgraphic newspaper cameras flashing, Lizzie Tilford walked out of her door between Provincial Police Inspector E.D.L. Hammond and Constable John Clark, on her way to be booked for murder and lodged in the Oxford County Jail. Soon the midnight shovels were busy again, this time digging up what remained of Lizzie's second husband, William Walker. No poison was found, though to this day you won't convince some people in Woodstock that he was not murdered. Especially after Mrs. Lily Macdougall told how, shortly before Walker's death, when she was complaining to Lizzie that her husband was ill and giving her trouble, Lizzie gave her a folk remedy to deal with the problem. 'That will fix him,' Lizzie had said. 'You'll soon be rid of him.'

For most of the trial, which began in September, Lizzie maintained a cool front, studiously taking notes as, day after day, the web of guilt was spun around her. Her composure cracked only when Tyrrell's sister, Annie, described the scene in the kitchen, when Tyrrell had cried, 'You have killed two and you will kill no more.'

'She has done nothing but tell lies,' Lizzie shrieked as Annie Tilford left the witness box. 'I can't go on. May God have mercy on my kids.' She then collapsed and had to be helped from the courtroom.

The one thing lacking in the prosecution's case was a motive. An insurance agent testified that Lizzie had called him several weeks before Tyrrell died to check how much he was insured for. It was only three hundred dollars — about the same amount there'd been on William Walker's life, and barely enough to cover funeral expenses. Tyrrell

103

brought in so little money that Lizzie and her son, William Walker, Jr., had to contribute to the household expenses, and some welfare assistance was needed for them to get by. Nevertheless, Agnes Allen, another of Tyrrell's legion of brothers and sisters, testified that, when she and her husband were visiting shortly before Tyrrell died, Lizzie asked them to help her write out his will, which left everything to Lizzie.

The druggist, Keith, had told of Lizzie coming into his store once and asking for empty capsules into which she would put a product she was using for slimming. Now, Mrs. Allen recalled Lizzie coming out of Tyrrell's bedroom with a capsule that she said her husband hadn't been able to keep down. Lizzie opened the top of the wood stove and threw the contents into the fire.

Things already looked bad for Lizzie when the prosecution produced a surprise witness. Mrs. Catherine Argent was the friend whose birthday party Lizzie had attended on the day the arsenic was delivered. Lizzie had brought an angel cake to the party, and no, said Mrs. Argent, no one had suffered any ill-effects after the party. But, while there, Lizzie made a phone call — possibly to the drug store to make sure the arsenic had been delivered while she was away from home — and had also received a phone call, apparently from Isabella. 'I ordered some arsenic,' Lizzie told her friend, 'and Bella (Isabella) is frightened to death to accept it.' On the day Tyrrell died, she phoned Mrs. Argent. 'Tyrrell's passed out,' she said. 'You remember that arsenic?' That was as much as she said.

A month after Tyrrell's death, Isabella brought her a

note from her mother: 'The provincial police have been to see Bella and she has told them I came to your house about one o'clock and left around five. Don't get mixed up in this. Burn.' Instead of burning the note, Mrs. Argent put it carefully away.

A brilliant October sun was streaming through the courtroom windows as the all-male jury filed out to consider its verdict. The public gallery was packed with women, some knitting, some drinking from flasks of coffee, none willing to risk going outside for fear of losing her seat. No woman had been hanged in Ontario for sixty years, juries having always bent over backwards to give a female accused the benefit of the doubt. Most people expected that Lizzie Tilford, too, would be spared the gallows.

As the afternoon wore on, the muted cheers of a crowd watching a lawn-bowling tournament outside the courtroom wafted through the open windows. Finally, at 8:30 p.m., the jury filed back in, and the foreman delivered the verdict: guilty. Lizzie sagged forward with a cry.

'. . . and thence be taken to a place of lawful execution . . .' intoned the judge.

'Oh, my God, it is not right, not fair,' she cried. 'Oh, your Lordship, I've been framed, framed! May God have mercy on the Tilfords' souls,' she wailed, then slumped in her seat.

'. . . and there be hanged by the neck until you are dead,' concluded the judge, as women cried and moaned. 'And may God have mercy on your soul.'

In the Oxford County Jail, Lizzie, once she was over the initial shock, busied herself knitting small items such as baby bootees, which were snapped up by souvenir hunters when they were put on sale at a charity bazaar. The Woodstock Ministerial Association asked that her death sentence be commuted or, at the very least, postponed, since the December 17 execution would cast a gloom over the Christmas season.

On November 30, an enterprising reporter from the *Detroit Times*, Dorothy Williams, fooled the sheriff at the jail into believing she was from the office of Lizzie's defence lawyer, and got in to interview the condemned woman. She described Lizzie as a tall, poised woman with an attractive, fresh English complexion and with short, greying blonde hair brushed straight back. The only softening touches in the vaulted whitewashed death cell were the rocking chair in which Lizzie sat and a pink begonia in a blue and white pot.

Lizzie, though she had forgone her chance to testify at her trial, was now insisting she was innocent. 'Gossip put me in this cell,' she told Williams. 'They said I wanted to get rid of my husband to marry William Blake. That's a lie. Blake was a friend of my son, Norman. He didn't mean anything to me. He always called me "Mom." I read his fortune one day and he discovered he could see into the future too.'

Blake, forty-two, was by then calling himself 'professor' and was telling fortunes in Toronto. But Lizzie was showing signs of disillusionment with the occult. 'I never saw this kind of death for myself in the tea leaves,' she said, puzzled.

In a small town, neither life nor death is anonymous, as is the case in a big city. Many of the people who gathered outside the jail on the night of December 17 had had their fortunes told by Lizzie Tilford or knew her from church. Mrs. Chris Clark, eighty-seven when I spoke to her, has memories as fresh as yesterday of the events following the arrest of Lizzie by her husband, Constable John Clark. Mrs. Clark worked several relief shifts guarding Lizzie in the death cell as a prison matron, and the hangman, a prison guard from Toronto who used the name Sam Edwards, stayed with her and her husband for several days while he prepared his equipment. He didn't seem at all upset at the prospect of hanging a woman, she said.

Others were more squeamish. A *Toronto Star* columnist argued that Lizzie should be spared on the odd grounds that, having attracted three husbands, she was not devoid of womanly qualities, and that her work for the Salvation Army indicated that there was a worthy Jekyll side to her character, 'as well as a peculiarly atrocious element of Hyde.' His final plea was 'that she should be saved from this horrible death simply because she is a woman. This whole judicial machinery has been devised by men and is carried out by men; women have a very slight part in it; and the debt of men to women is so vast that to exempt women from the death penalty is a very slight expression of their obligation.'

There was, in the event, no last-minute reprieve. Snow was falling as Lizzie, who had refused an injection of morphine, walked bareheaded across the prison yard to the scaffold. She was finally lost for words as the black hood was pulled over her head, and her arms and feet were secured. Only forty-five seconds elapsed from the moment she emerged from the jail until the telltale thud of the trapdoor.

I am not entirely convinced that was the last of Lizzie. She had dealt in the occult, and something of her fearsome personality still seems to linger around Woodstock. Certainly when I mentioned her name to Victor King who delivered the arsenic and who had once had his fortune told by Lizzie, his hands shook violently. King, sixty-five, was living in a senior citizens' home not two hundred yards from the cemetery where Lizzie is buried. 'She was an uneducated, lower class of person,' he spat out. 'I guess I feel she got her just desserts.'

And the Tilfords haven't changed their view. 'Oh, she poisoned more than one husband, I'm sure of that,' said one of the Tilford women guardedly from behind her screen door.

But there were still her children and a handful of friends left to gather by the light of car headlights and flashlights for the funeral in the Baptist cemetery shortly after the execution. The Reverend Stanley Baker conducted the burial service and − Lizzie had left him her Seth Parker Hymnal, suitably inscribed, as a token of gratitude − then her coffin was lowered into the ground beside the recently disturbed remains of her second husband, William Walker, who, having died from natural causes, had no reason to bear a grudge. Or had he?

I'LL TAKE CARE
OF IT, MOTHER

What was the sin of John F. Yuhas? What offence had the apparently inoffensive Yuhas, retired and tubercular at age fifty-seven, committed that four of the women closest to him – and one man besides – would be implicated in his murder? Examining a photograph of him we see a man obviously wasted by disease, his collar many sizes too large for him, a benign-looking man, a smile touching a mouth that could only be called generous.

He was, we learn, a quiet man. His neighbours on upper-middle-class Coolidge Road in South Buffalo, New York, didn't even know his name, although he sometimes helped them start their cars in cold weather. His only known indulgence was a game of golf four or five times a week. Yuhas would normally have been on the links that Sunday morning, August 24, 1975. His wife, Mona, in fact told the police that when she woke up about 10:00 a.m. and found her husband not at home, she assumed he had got up early, as he often did, taken his clubs and gone golfing.

An hour later, Mona Yuhas, along with her sister,

Margaret Alvey, approached State Trooper Bruce Pagels who was assisting another motorist on the thruway not far from the Yuhas home. She was worried, she said, because her husband had not returned from his golf game, and his car appeared to be abandoned on the shoulder of the highway. While Mrs. Yuhas watched, Officer Pagels examined the inside of the car, finding papers strewn around and, on the floor, the keys to the car.

'Why don't you look in the trunk?' she suggested. 'Maybe his clothes are there.' Pagels put the key in the lock, turned it and lifted the lid. Then he slammed it down very quickly. For a long time afterwards he would not forget the sight of John Yuhas's emaciated and bloodied face staring up at him.

Was Yuhas the victim of a thruway attack by thieves, as it first appeared? If so, his assailants had been shockingly thorough. The post mortem showed that Yuhas had first been beaten about the face and head with a blunt instrument, then stabbed seven times in the body, and finally shot three times in the face.

And if it wasn't a random attack, then what was the point, wondered Homicide Chief Leo J. Donovan of the Buffalo police force as he watched the gruesome post mortem later that day. Even a layman could see John Yuhas was so ravaged by tuberculosis he would likely have been dead in a few months' time.

The answer, he concluded, must lie in the handsome, two-storey colonial-style house on Coolidge Road in which Yuhas had lived so unobtrusively. It was, Donovan recalls, a comfortable old house, rented from a doctor who, two years earlier, had had his office and living quarters there.

110

Everything appeared to be in order, but when Donovan announced he and his men wanted to search upstairs, Mona Yuhas's seventy-year-old mother, Gladys Pounds, who lived with the couple and who actually paid the rent on the house, seemed put out. In fact, said Donovan, the imperious old lady came clattering up the stairs after them, demanding, 'What business do you have here?' and was so angry she dropped her walking cane.

Since becoming ill, John Yuhas had slept in an upstairs den in a special hospital bed. The room looked tidy; then an officer, bending down, noticed blood splatters on the wall beneath the dresser. The bed was made, but when the mattress was turned over, bloodstains and a bullet hole were revealed on its underside. On closer examination, the homicide officers found a trail of blood spots, which someone had tried unsuccessfully to remove, leading from the bedroom down the stairs and into the garage.

No, they knew nothing about that, insisted the two women. Mona Yuhas still claimed she had heard nothing and that, as far as she knew, her husband had left home that morning to play golf.

But, plainly, something very peculiar had been going on at the Yuhas house in the early hours of Sunday. A young woman happening to pass the house at about 3:30 a.m. noticed a woman with red hair open the front door and close it very quickly. A moment later, the witness saw the same woman, who was wearing a blouse, dungarees and, oddly, a pair of black gloves, peeking out of the front window. 'I thought someone was robbing the house,' she would later testify.

111

When the young woman's boyfriend, Kevin Higgins (whom she would soon after marry), picked her up in his car a few minutes later, she told him of the strange goings-on. They returned to the house together and knocked at the front door. 'I think someone's robbing your house,' Colleen told the middle-aged woman who answered the door. 'There's nothing going on around here,' the woman replied.

At that moment, Colleen noticed the redhead sitting in a car in the driveway. The woman came over to her, very upset, and said she had been smoking grass in what used to be the doctor's office at the front of the house, and didn't want her mother to know. Just then a woman Colleen would later recognize as John Yuhas's widow came out, inquiring what was going on.

'There's nothing going on here, is there, Sis?' said the woman who had originally answered the door. 'No,' replied the other.

The vignette ended with a passing police car slowing down. 'Anything going on?' called an officer, but he didn't stop.

Mrs. Yuhas had some explaining to do, and at the police station, after a troubling interview with a lie-detector technician, she changed her story. Sunday night had started out little different from any other night at the Yuhas house, she said. Her husband had been watching television, until his mother-in-law came into the room and, as usual, he retired to the basement. Her husband and Mrs. Pounds, her mother, got along so badly that they could not bear to be in the same room together, she explained.

When her mother went to bed at about 10:00 p.m., John re-emerged from the basement and watched with Mona and her sister, Margaret, who was visiting. An hour later, John went to the kitchen, made coffee, and they all watched the news together. Mona and John then observed their nightly ritual of taking their sleeping pills together and, while her husband became sleepy right away and went to bed after giving her a kiss, she stayed up to watch the late movie in the living room with Margaret. About 1:00 a.m. or 1:30 a.m., Margaret's daughter, Linda Lee Smith, arrived with her boyfriend, Jim Butler. The cast in this grim drama was finally assembled.

If the plot to kill John Yuhas had a beginning, it was a phone call that took place about a month earlier. Mona Yuhas told the police that she had been listening in on a call her mother made to Margaret, who was then living in Whiting, Indiana. A strange family, you would say, where people listened in on other people's phone calls, but perhaps Mona had her reasons.

Gladys, a retired stenographer, was playing a tired, worn-out record as far as Mona was concerned, running down her son-in-law and telling Margaret how she just couldn't stand the man. In fact, she said, she would like to have him killed. Could Margaret be of any help? 'I'll take care of it, Mother,' Margaret replied. 'I know someone who will do it.'

'I'll pay a thousand dollars,' said the older woman. 'And while he's at it, maybe he could kill Wayne too.' Wayne was another of Mrs. Pounds's sons-in-law, living in Pennsylvania. She didn't like him either.

After overhearing such remarks, one would have

expected Mona Yuhas would consider calling the police or having her mother committed to a mental institution. At the very least, one would think, she would have warned her husband. She didn't. She said she told her nephew, Clayton Pounds, but he didn't take the threat seriously, so she let the matter drop.

And maybe she didn't make the connection when, shortly afterwards, Margaret called to say that her daughter, Linda, was moving to Buffalo from Indiana with her boyfriend, Jim Butler. 'Can you help them get settled?' she asked. 'He's such a nice boy.'

Not so nice according to police in Illinois and Indiana, who, at that time, had fugitive warrants out for Butler for attempted murder and assault. Jim, thirty-five, slim, with dark hair, heavy eyebrows and a pencil moustache, arrived in Buffalo the last week of July and stayed at the Yuhas home the first week. Mona would later say: 'I took him out myself and found him an apartment, and my husband took him the following day and got him a job. But he only lasted there part of the first day. They let him go because he gave them an assumed name.'

Linda Lee Smith would confirm that, with her four children, she had joined Butler at the apartment for which 'Grandma paid the rent.' Oh yes, she knew all about the murder plot. Her mother had told her that Grandma had called, looking for a hit man. Margaret had told Jim, too, and he said he knew someone who would do the job. There must have been other conversations, but all we know is that, soon after midnight on August 25, Linda and Jim got into her mother's 1972 Mercury Monterey and drove from their place on Dearborn Street in Buffalo

114

Elizabeth Marina Jones

Ruth Ellis – described by a jury
member after her trial as 'a common
little West End tart' (*Hulton Picture
Company*)

A crowd stands in silent protest outside Holloway prison at 9 a.m. on 13
July 1955, the morning Ruth Ellis was hanged (*Syndication International*)

Jean Harris leaves Westchester
County Courthouse, 2 April 1981
(*Popperfoto*)

Gladys Pounds. 'Grandma had
called, looking for a hit man.'
(*Buffalo Evening News*)

Clara Ford's trial hits the headlines

Madame Marie Marguerite Fahmy
(*Popperfoto*)

Myra Hindley at the time of her
arrest (*Camera Press*)

Myra Hindley, aged 44, with the
prison governor's two white-haired
terriers inside the grounds of
Cookham Wood Prison, 1989
(*Camera Press*)

Saddleworth Moor where the bodies of Lesley Ann Downey, John
Kilbride and, later, Pauline Reade were found. Keith Bennett's body has
yet to be discovered (*Hulton Picture Company*)

A publicity photograph of 'Lozanne', the name under which Alma Rattenbury published her songs (*Hulton Picture Company*)

Alma Rattenbury was booed loudly as she left the Old Bailey after being found not guilty of murder (*Hulton Picture Company*)

Florence Elizabeth Chandler Maybrick in 1904, after her release from prison

Florence Bravo at the time of her marriage to Charles Bravo (*Hulton Picture Company*)

A sketch in court of the inquiry into Charles Bravo's death – Mrs Cox is cross-examined by Mr Lewis (*Hulton Picture Company*)

A full-page newspaper illustration of the time satisfied public opinion against Louise Masset by showing her being prepared for execution

Katie Harper is led away from court after being convicted of the murder of her first husband 23 years earlier (*Winnipeg Sun*)

to the house on Coolidge Road, where they found Mona and Margaret watching television in the living room.

The people of Buffalo are not surprised by murder. Leo Donovan says that, prior to his retirement, he alone investigated a couple of thousand homicides, some involving unbelievable brutality, and with motives running the gamut of human emotions. But, when Buffalo newspaper readers turned to their front pages on August 26, 1975, they knew the Yuhas case was one for the books.

There they learned that four women and a man had been charged in John Yuhas's murder. Gladys Pounds, his mother-in-law, was charged with first-degree conspiracy and criminal solicitation; Margaret Alvey, his sister-in-law, and Linda Lee Smith, his niece, were both charged with first-degree conspiracy and criminal facilitation; Mona L. Yuhas, his widow, was charged with obstructing government administration; and James F. Butler faced charges of murder, first-degree conspiracy and possession of a weapon.

'We called the case "All in the family," ' said Donovan dryly.

But if this unholy family stood together, who was there to point the finger? The very nature of a conspiracy, after all, is that the participants act together in secrecy. Three days later, Buffalo had its answer. The charge against Mona Yuhas, not a very serious one in any case, was dismissed. Mrs. Yuhas would now testify for the prosecution.

And so, by a strange twist, Mona Yuhas moved out of the now-notorious house on Coolidge Road and into a condominium apartment in suburban Cheektowaga,

115

which she shared with Gladys Pounds, now out on bail and waiting to be tried as the person who had instigated the murder plot against her husband.

What did they talk about, these two women? Or did they just watch TV, take their sleeping pills and retire, always avoiding the terrible subject. That they were under pressure, there can be no doubt. In October, with Mona at the wheel, their car went into the back of a parked tractor-trailer, and both women were taken to hospital. In April, a month before Mrs. Pounds was to go on trial, the rescue squad was summoned to the women's apartment. Mrs. Pounds had supposedly fallen out of bed. After putting her back in bed, rescue workers noticed a strong medicinal odour. A few days later, Mrs. Pounds's son, Jack, checking the apartment, found his sister, Mona, lying unconscious in the hallway. His mother was lying dead on her bedroom floor. Both women had taken overdoses of sleeping pills; both had left suicide notes.

'Margaret, Linda and James Butler killed John and please see they go to jail for it,' Mona had written in her note. 'Linda beat me, Margaret gave me something to knock me out and James Butler killed Dady [sic].'

With Mrs. Yuhas in poor condition in Meyer Memorial Hospital, state prosecutors saw their cases against the three defendants in the murder going out of the window. 'If she dies,' Assistant District Attorney Timothy J. Drury was quoted in the newspaper as saying, 'we'll have to take a long hard look at the case.' Mona Yuhas recovered, but Drury's remarks had not gone unnoticed. Just days before she was due to testify in the trial of her niece, Linda Smith, Mona went missing. Her abandoned car was found near her sister Margaret's home. Police were baffled. Was it suicide or foul play?

A nationwide bulletin was issued for Mona Yuhas. Meanwhile Linda Smith went on the witness stand and denied earlier statements she had made to the police that implicated her in the murder; after deliberating for eight and a half hours, the jury found her not guilty. The verdict might have been different if Mona Yuhas had gone into the witness box, admitted one juror.

A month after she'd gone missing, Mrs. Yuhas was arrested by the FBI at her brother-in-law's home in Owensboro, Kentucky. For much of the time, she had been hiding out in Las Vegas after her sister Margaret, according to police, arranged her getaway.

But the prosecution had not given up on Linda Lee Smith. Having been found not guilty of murder, she was ordered to stand trial on conspiracy charges. And, finally, almost exactly a year after John Yuhas's body had been found, his widow went into the box at Linda's trial and gave a jury her version of that night's events.

When Linda and Jim arrived that night, she said, she had gone to bed. 'I don't know what time it was, but I was woken out of my sleep with my husband hollering, "What are you doing in my room!" I heard a noise like someone beating him up.' She was just coming out of her bedroom door, when Linda, wearing black gloves up to her elbows, grabbed her, leaving bruises on her arms, and shoved her back into her bed.

'I was hollering, "Let him go, Let him go" and then I heard my husband holler, "Oh, my God!" ' As she jumped out of bed again, her niece grabbed her and

117

shoved her into her mother's room and told her that if she didn't keep quiet, everyone in the house would be killed. 'And don't forget you have four grandchildren,' Linda told her aunt. In the hallway Mona got a glimpse through the bedroom door of Jim Butler on top of her husband, stabbing him. At some point that night, she said, Jim Butler put his arms around her and said, 'Aunt Mona, you are going to be a lot happier now. This should have been done a long time ago.' 'I'm not your aunt,' she'd snapped.

She stayed in her mother's bed, 'and then I heard a noise like thump, thump thump, going down the stairs.' Where was Mrs. Pounds all this time? 'My mother was sleeping. She is hard of hearing.'

Linda Lee Smith had told police that, after 'Aunt Mona' went up to bed, her boyfriend took out a gun he had used to threaten her in the past and laid it on the coffee table. 'Be cool,' he told her and her mother. 'Don't go to pieces. Everything will be all right. I'm for real.' 'I knew that by that phrase he meant he was going to kill Uncle John,' she said. Then he had gone upstairs, carrying a sawed-off billiard cue, which, said Linda, she had found and into which she had burned the names of her four children.

After hearing several thumps from upstairs and her aunt crying out, 'Leave him alone,' said Linda, she had rushed up and pushed her back into her room, saying, she claimed, 'Don't cry, Aunt Mona, don't cry.' In her uncle's bedroom, she said, she had seen Jim sitting with his back to her and blood all over the floor. Shortly after, she said, 'I saw Jim carrying Uncle John out into the

118

garage on his shoulder. He was wrapped in a white blanket and blood was dripping down from the blanket.'

'Don't just stand there,' her boyfriend yelled at her, 'start cleaning up.' While she washed the dark red stains out of the rug on the stairs, she said, her mother was on her hands and knees, cleaning the carpet in front of John Yuhas's bedroom. It was when Jim told her to go and wait outside for him in her mother's car that the young couple had come to the door to report that they believed that a robbery was taking place.

Their cleaning chores completed, mother and daughter waited in the car until Jim Butler emerged with two plastic garbage bags containing the blood-soiled bedding and cleaning materials, and put them in the back seat. 'Pretty good,' he said, patting Linda on the leg.

Linda followed Jim and her mother, who were in John Yuhas's car, through the silent streets and on to the thruway, where Jim parked. At that point, Margaret Alvey would say, Jim opened the trunk of the car, and she heard 'two shots that sounded like a kid's toy gun.' On the way home in Linda's car, they stopped to throw the gun over a bridge and again to leave the plastic bags in a dumpster.

It was all so matter-of-fact, as if the women had simply been disposing of a couch that didn't match the living-room suite. What had gone on that made the removal of John Yuhas, a dying man, so important?

Her mother, testified Mona, had lived with them for nine years and 'was always picking on my husband and wished him dead lots of times.' Had she told her husband of the murder plot? 'He wouldn't have believed it,' she replied. 'He would have laughed at me. He thought too much of my mother even though they didn't get along.'

Their son, John Yuhas, Jr., would testify that, in the bickering, 'she never took my father's side. She was more for her mother.' Shortly before he was murdered, his father told him he couldn't stand the hassle any more and was thinking of leaving the state. 'I wanted my father around because I loved him a lot,' said the son.

And the motive, apart from the pure spite of Gladys Pounds? Mona Yuhas admitted she had collected a total of $7,500 on her husband's life-insurance policies. The women, said Homicide Chief Donovan, had discussed how they might spruce up the house if they collected that money.

Giving her testimony, Mona Yuhas never once looked at her niece. As if to placate her, she said, 'My niece is a very nice girl and I always loved her. Jim was a nice boy too,' she added gratuitously. 'He was clean, polite and he never swore. '

Linda Smith was not consoled. 'To think,' she said indignantly after her aunt stepped down from the witness box, 'that I am still writing to her and that I bought her the clothes she was wearing today!'

This time it took the jury only ten minutes to find Linda Smith guilty of conspiracy, and she received a sentence of from eight to twenty-five years. Her mother, Margaret Alvey, pleaded guilty to the same offence and received an identical sentence; Jim Butler, the clumsy hit man, was convicted of murder and given a term of twenty-five years.

The original culprit, Gladys Pounds, was beyond the reach of earthly courts. 'She was the one who was boss in that house,' said Donovan. But, when it came down to it, no one in that house was willing to stand up for John Yuhas's right to live, and so he died a miserable and bloody death.

Among the ranks of mothers-in-law, who, by reputation, are known for their tartness, Gladys Pounds was, indeed, larger than life. She was not, however, unique. In 1989, Mrs. Lee Goldsmith was charged in Florida with hiring a hit man − actually an undercover police officer − and paying him $9,500 to kill her son-in-law of four years, David Brownstein, whom she described as 'short, fat and dirty.' Paying off the officer under the impression the execution had been carried out, Mrs. Goldsmith said, 'He was asking for it, he got it.' She was sentenced to five and a half years in prison.

WHEREVER HE HAS GONE,
I HAVE GONE

There is still another body buried up here somewhere on Saddleworth Moor. It's that of Keith Bennett who was twelve when he disappeared one day in 1964. He'll probably never be found now, unless the moor disgorges his body the way it did that of ten-year-old Lesley Downey. And that would not be so surprising: scrambling up the slope toward the Stonehenge-like stand of boulders that dominates this desolate landscape, it seems to me that the moor is in a permanent state of upheaval. Water gurgles beneath the grass, and several times, as I jump the streams that expose the black peat beneath, like open wounds, I trip and slide cursing into the gullies. Forget any notion of the romantic moors of the Brontës: Saddleworth Moor, just outside Manchester, is about as beautiful as an open-cast mine. As Joe Mounsey, who saw more than enough of it when he was up here on the long body search, told me, 'It's the surface of the bloody moon up there.'

In that sense Saddleworth Moor differs from most scenes of notorious murders, which turn out to be banal

– tacky suburban bungalows, tired and shabby rooming houses, neat backyards with bodies planted behind the cabbages. Even if you didn't know what happened here, I suspect Saddleworth would inspire a prickle of fear, a sense that anything could happen here. And did.

Ian Brady and Myra Hindley disposed of four of their five young victims on this moor. In terms of the sheer number killed, Hindley and Brady are not in the same league as the Ted Bundy-type serial killer who has emerged in the last two decades. But, in terms of horror, their crimes are matched only by the Manson murders in California, and for a simple reason: the Manson case, in which the mostly female followers of Charles Manson slaughtered the pregnant actress Sharon Tate and eight others, and the Moors Murders have changed our ideas about what women are capable of. What has aroused unprecedented loathing for Myra Hindley – and what keeps her still behind bars at the time of writing twenty-five years later – is the revulsion people feel at the idea that an apparently ordinary young woman could entice children away and participate in their violation and murder, helping to photograph and tape-record their death agonies.

When Hindley said of her partnership with Brady, 'Wherever he has gone, I have gone, and he has never been anywhere without me,' she was not just alluding to the fact that she drove the car when they were hunting prey or disposing of bodies. Hers is the disturbing and final assertion of female equality. In spite of the assertions of Colin Wilson (in *A Criminal History of Mankind*) and others that Hindley was a 'devoted slave,' a dupe of

124

Brady, I believe her participation went beyond that into a savage enjoyment of these barbarous killings.

Brady had the kind of background you'd expect of a pathological child killer. His mother, single at the time, put an advertisement in a store window when he was three months old: 'Working woman willing to have child adopted,' and he was brought up by an older couple in Glasgow's rough Gorbals neighbourhood. From early on, young Ian had a cruel streak: friends remembered him burying a cat alive in a graveyard. His persistent thievery put him in a Borstal institution for young offenders in his mid-teens.

But, by his early twenties, after a few dead-end jobs and a few more brushes with the law, Brady decided to adopt at least a facade of respectability. He studied accounting and, in February 1959, he applied for a job as a clerk with a small chemical and soap company in Gorton, part of Greater Manchester. But the clerk who impressed people with his haughty manner at work was amusing himself nights reading *Pleasures of the Torture Chamber* and *Those About to Die* and collecting Nazi memorabilia.

Hindley's upbringing, by contrast, you'd almost call sweet. Born into a cheerful, extended, working-class Manchester family, she was a stocky, determined little girl who spent as much time with her Gran next door, who doted on her, as she did with her parents. Of a little above average intelligence, she enjoyed a normal-enough childhood – with the exception of one incident. When she was fifteen, Myra befriended a boy named Michael Higgins, two years younger than herself, and protected

125

him against bullies. One hot June day, Michael asked Myra to go swimming to the reservoir, but she couldn't be bothered. He was not home by supper, and Myra was in the crowd that watched his body being pulled from the slimy water. If only she'd gone, it would never have happened, she told herself, and for a long time afterwards she was a different girl – silent, withdrawn, going about in black and blaming herself for Michael's death.

There were boyfriends, but she didn't come across for them. A bit old-fashioned, people thought her, saving herself for the right fellow. Meanwhile she enjoyed baby-sitting, picturing what it would be like to have kids of her own. Then, in January 1961, she started a new job as a typist with a small Gorton firm, and was soon noticing the stand-offish fellow with the Scottish accent who worked in his own office. His name: Ian Brady.

For months she watched him, waiting for him to make a move. Her diary for the period is almost school-girlish: 'Aug. 2, Not sure if he likes me. Aug. 14, He has a cold and I would love to mother him. Aug. 29, I hope he loves me and will marry me some day.' She spied on him, noting when he got phone calls in the office, discovering by October that he lived with his parents and rarely went out. It wasn't until just before Christmas that she noted triumphantly: 'Out with Ian.'

After seeing in the New Year at her parents' home with a bottle of whisky Brady had bought, they returned to her grandmother's house, where Hindley lived. The light upstairs was out. Her Gran had gone to bed.

She thought her great romance had finally begun. She

was wrong. It was her education that was beginning. He tried out his German on her, got her to pose for him, while he tried to take porno pictures like those in the magazines he had, and introduced her to the pain-pleasure-pain world of the Marquis de Sade. He got her to buy two handguns, and weekends they would rent a car – a little station wagon with a fold-down seat and doors in the back – which Hindley always drove.

By November 23, 1963, when the newspapers were full of the assassination of President John F. Kennedy in Dallas the day before, he judged her ready. Did they talk about what they were going to do? Did she really believe him that day when he sent her to buy a shovel in a hardware store and said it was for digging peat on the moor for Gran's fireplace? As they sat in their rented car in Ashton Market that Saturday afternoon, watching for an unaccompanied child, was Myra Hindley, the baby-sitter who loved children, the girl who had grieved for Michael Higgins, the one who was devastated by the death of Gran's dog – was that Myra Hindley already dead and gone?

And then John Kilbride, twelve, lingering too long at the market, knowing he'd be late getting home for his tea and likely to catch it, came walking by. A lift? He climbed in beside the kind lady and gentleman who had asked him. His mother had never told him not to talk to kind ladies.

The hue and cry was huge: large headlines, posters marked 'Have you seen this child?', organized searches, false clues, dashed hopes. Then, gradually, people forgot about John Kilbride. And on August 15, 1964, when all

127

the hullabaloo had died down, Ian Brady married Myra Hindley quietly at the All Saints registry office.

Of course, John Kilbride's mother could not, would not, ever forget. When, late the following year, Detective Chief Inspector Joe Mounsey was assigned to Ashton-under-Lyne, John was still listed as missing, and he went to see John's mother, who lived in the district. 'It was a missing child,' Mounsey, sixty-four and retired, explained simply when I went to see him. But he'll never forget Sheila Kilbride. 'She was a very gracious lady,' he said, his face softening. Mounsey will tell you he was the son of a policeman but joined the force, following wartime military service, only 'for something to do.' One suspects that there must have been more to it than that; he made inspector in his thirties.

I pressed him on why police work had become his obsession. 'I recognized,' he said at last, 'that there are victims, too many damn victims. And many of the victims are physically weaker. It's true − the strong do oppress the weak.' And as if to conceal the strength of his emotions he made a show of scolding Bill, the Staffordshire bull terrier his colleagues had given him on retirement, picked, I suspect, because Bill's features resemble Mounsey's.

After the first time, Mounsey called regularly on the Kilbrides. Not that he had any news, but at least they knew he hadn't forgotten. It wasn't until two years later that Mounsey's phone rang and Superintendent Robert Talbot told him he had a piece of paper in front of him that they'd found in the home of a couple going by the names of Ian Brady and Myra Hindley. On the paper were a number of names of film stars and such; one of the names was John Kilbride.

The arrest of Hindley and Brady occurred following a scene only Dostoevsky could have imagined. The couple had been bringing along David Smith, Myra's teenaged brother-in-law, married to her sister Maureen, introducing him to *Mein Kampf*, de Sade, and the whole literature of torture and sadism. Smith, who had been in trouble with the law in a minor way, seemed a likely candidate to join them in their bizarre exploits.

About 6:15 p.m., on October 6, 1965, Smith was around, borrowing some tea at the new house Hindley and Brady had recently moved into with Myra's Gran on Wardle Brook Avenue in Hyde, another district of Manchester. The couple was just going out, and Smith would remember that Myra was smartly turned out in a leopard-pattern dress and white high heels, and was carrying a large, unwieldy handbag — in it, in fact, were two guns. Also, she was holding an odd item to be taking along on an evening out — a pair of binoculars.

Smith returned to the flat around the corner that he shared with Maureen and went back to reading *Fanny Hill*. At 11:40, they were in bed reading, when the buzzer went from the lobby. It was Myra. Smith was pulling on some clothes when she came in. The first thing he noticed was that her makeup was smudged, her hair a mess, and she had on the sloppy skirt and sweater she'd only wear at home on weekends. After chatting a bit, she asked her sister to tell their mother when she saw her that Myra would be over Monday night to bleach her hair for her. Was that all she'd come for so late at night? Anyway,

129

would Dave see her home through the houses? 'It's dark and I'm scared,' she said. But hadn't she walked over a few minutes before on her own? Smith got on his jacket and took up the special stick he used when walking the dog. But he shouldn't bring the dog, said Hindley, because he was sure to fight with hers.

Outside her house, a few minutes later, Hindley asked him to wait across the street, 'in case Ian's doing something,' like taping a record. She'd flick on the landing light if it was okay for him to come in. He waited a few minutes and then the light was flicked on twice. When he tapped on the front door, Brady opened it. 'Hello, want to see those miniature bottles?' he said, referring to an earlier conversation they'd had and speaking in an unnaturally, loud cheerful voice, as if he wanted someone in the sitting room to hear. Brady went light-footedly up the stairs and returned in a moment with some small bottles of liqueur, which he set on the kitchen table before going into the living room, leaving the door ajar.

Only a few seconds had passed when Smith heard a scream from the other room and Myra shouting, 'Dave, help him! Help him!' He grabbed his stick, which he'd brought with him after all, and ran into the room, thinking Brady was being attacked. By the subdued light of the small lamp on the television set he could just make out Brady smashing down the blunt side of an axe on an object on the floor. It must be a joke they were playing on him. His mouth formed a smile. What did they think he was, stupid? That thing on the floor, it must be a store dummy or something of the sort. It couldn't be human.

130

But the screaming was coming from the object on the floor, and, as Smith watched, the figure writhed in agony and cowered away from the blows. It was Edward Evans, a seventeen-year-old youth Brady had once seen in a gay bar and had picked up at a railway buffet earlier in the evening.

Smith was traumatized. Running seemed out of the question. Fourteen times the axe came down on the helpless figure, who at first tried to crawl away. Then the screaming, the gurgling, the writhing stopped and Brady said, 'He's a goner. We'll have to get rid of him.' As if this was a chore he was used to, he took a cushion cover and pulled it over the pulped remains of Evans's head and drew a length of electric cord around the neck.

Smith actually visualized himself running like a mad thing out into the night and home to Maureen, but instead, he stood glued to the floor, held by the look in Brady's hard, cold eyes. 'Here, Dave,' he said, handing him the axe. 'Feel the weight of that.' Smith, in a trance, took hold of the still dripping axe, implicating himself now in the killing. Brady took it back from him and laid it on the body.

'This was the messiest yet,' he said, wiping his hands on a magazine. 'It normally only takes one blow.'

'Myra!' The voice came from upstairs, thin and querulous. Hindley went to the bottom of the stairs. ''It's just the dog barking,' she called up to her Gran, who had been wakened by the noise.

'Get cleaning stuff and rags,' Brady told her when she returned to the sitting room. While Brady and Hindley scrubbed the floor and walls, Smith, following Brady's instructions, carefully wiped all the drips of blood off the bars of the budgie cage. Nothing was said about the cadaver lying on the floor, and they cleaned around it. Then briskly, like a duty nurse coping with a messy emergency, Hindley fetched a blanket, a sheet and a roll of semi-transparent plastic sheeting kept in the kitchen. Brady laid them on the floor and, with Smith holding the feet while he grabbed under the armpits, they placed the body on the sheet. Hindley returned with water to clean the spot where the head had been. Oh, one thing they'd forgotten, said Brady: they didn't have any string. The cord on Smith's dog stick would do. Smith cut it free and handed it over, not thinking that again he was implicating himself in the murder.

With the corpse parcelled, Brady and Hindley considered their options. Getting it to the car would mean walking past three houses. That wouldn't do. They'd put it upstairs, and the following day Smith could fetch a baby carriage from his grandfather's. They'd use that to get the body to the car before taking it up to the moors. While Hindley held the door of her grandmother's bedroom shut, the two men carried the unwieldy parcel up the stairs and down the hall to one of the other bedrooms.

With the night's work done, Hindley made them all a pot of tea. As she sat with her blood-stained slippers resting on the mantelpiece, she asked Brady if he remembered the time he'd been burying a body on the moors and a policeman, seeing her sitting in the car, had stopped and asked her, 'What's the trouble?' And she'd told him she was just waiting for the spark plugs to dry, and he'd driven off. What a lark! For her and Brady, the intoxication of the killing had not yet worn off. 'You could see the blow register in his eyes!' she said eagerly.

It was after three in the morning when they let Smith out of the front door. Once outside, he ran — but he could not escape what he had witnessed. He would never escape it. To this day, he wakes in cold sweats.

Once home, he went into the bathroom, splashed cold water on his face and was sick. He climbed into bed beside Maureen. 'What's the matter, love?' she said. 'Not feeling well?' Stumbling and stuttering, the cigarette shaking in his hand, he told her the whole story. What had he been drinking . . . or smoking? He must be mad. And then, she began to believe him.

It was getting light when, like two small, frightened animals, they crept out of their apartment building, Smith carrying a large screwdriver and a breadknife under his coat, which were somehow supposed to protect them. At the corner of the street, Smith went into a red phone box. It was 6:07 a.m. He dialled 999 and asked for the police.

But that was only the beginning. After the police arrived at the little house on Wardle Brook Avenue and discovered the obscene, plastic-wrapped parcel in the bedroom, Hindley and Brady weren't going to make it easy for anyone. Let the coppers find out what they bloody well could.

And they did. In the tiny station wagon the couple now owned, they found a neatly ruled plan in Brady's handwriting for abducting a man, murdering him and disposing of his body. Superintendent Talbot, riffling through mounds of junk from a wardrobe, found a list of names in an exercise book, some of them of film stars,

133

Joan Crawford and (misspelled) Alec Guineas. One stood out: John Kilbride. He dialled Joe Mounsey in Ashton-under-Lyne. 'I knew it would come,' said Mounsey. 'First thing in the morning? I'll be there.'

Smith had told the police Brady and Hindley had talked about killing people and burying them up on the moors. Mounsey asked Brady about that. It was just talk to impress young Smith, he insisted. And John Kilbride? He showed him the list of names in the exercise book. It was just the name of someone he'd known in school, said Brady. Mounsey thought of Sheila Kilbride, waiting, hoping.

Hindley corroborated Brady's story, offering blank-faced denials. 'She was a hard nut,' remembers Mounsey.

There were stacks of photographs seized at the house, some in a tartan-covered album, some snaps going back to when Brady and Hindley were kids. Mounsey was interested in the more recent ones, those taken on the moor. They showed Hindley and Brady in different settings, sometimes in front of rock formations, sometimes with the car. The chief inspector ordered blow-ups. Tomorrow, he said, they'd start digging.

Day after day, the buses climbed the steep hill to Saddleworth Moor, carrying the most dispirited, reluctant bunch of coppers ever assembled. As if the slogging hard work of the digging wasn't enough, they had to contend with the reporters with their smart-ass jokes and the photographers. One afternoon, when Mounsey said it was time to knock off, a rookie constable, only three days on the job and wondering if he'd joined the police force to be a ditch-digger, had a call of nature and asked to

134

be let off the bus before they started for home. They all laughed as the bashful youngster ran up the hill to get out of sight. They didn't laugh when they saw the expression on his face as he returned. He had seen a bone sticking out of the ground. It belonged to Lesley Ann Downey, who was ten when she disappeared on her way home from a Christmas fair on Boxing Day, 1964.

The police hadn't given up on the house yet either. Detective Chief Inspector Jack Tyrrell worried over that list of names in the exercise book, wondering if there could be another list they'd overlooked. He went back to Wardle Brook Avenue, let himself in and began the tedious business of going over every cranny in the house once again. Among the sex books and thrillers, one book struck him as out of place – a prayer book. Inside, it was inscribed, 'To Myra from Auntie Kath and Uncle Bert, 16 Nov. 1958, souvenir of her first communion.' Tyrrell bent back the covers, tipped it upside down, then noticed a slip of paper concealed in the spine of the book. It was a ticket from the left-luggage office at Central Station, Manchester.

For Mounsey, finding Lesley Ann Downey wasn't enough. His men kept digging away while he pored over the enlarged snapshots, trying to place the locations in that wild and almost featureless landscape. One photo in particular fascinated him. It showed Hindley crouching with her puppy nestled in her coat. Her half-smile seemed to be directed, not at the dog or the camera, but at the ground in front of her. The enlargement had brought into focus a distinctive group of rocks on the hilltop in the background.

135

Mounsey scanned the slope from every angle, but could never get the rocks properly framed. One day he crossed the road that meandered across the moor, went farther down the pitted, uneven slope, then looked back. He realized that, all along, he should have been viewing the rocks from a distance. Next morning he was back with a police photographer who set down his tripod and studied the scene through his viewfinder. Then he beckoned to Mounsey to take a look. It was exactly like the snapshot. Only Hindley and the dog were missing. By late morning, an officer poking a long, thin stick into the ground and then withdrawing it before sniffing the end, suddenly stopped, and sniffed again. They had found John Kilbride.

'I can remember how upset you were the night John Kilbride was found,' said Margaret Mounsey, who was a policewoman before she married Joe.

'It was police work,' said Mounsey gruffly as he rubbed Bill's throat. 'Maybe that's our cop-out as human beings. It wouldn't do to cry too much − spoil the evidence.'

The morning after the body was found, Mounsey called on Sheila Kilbride to get her to identify a shoe they'd found in the grave. Then he helped her arrange a funeral mass for John.

As I talked to him so many years after all these events, the old indignation came boiling out. He wanted to talk about the contents of the two suitcases they'd recovered from the left-luggage office. The nine photographs of a little girl, clearly Lesley Ann Downey, her mouth gagged with a man's scarf, her thin little body naked except for her shoes and socks. They'd posed her this way and that, and from the look on her face you could see that, in addition to being frightened, she was puzzled about what was going on.

And perhaps Myra Hindley could have claimed she wasn't there, didn't know what had happened, if it hadn't been for the tapes. There were two of them, and they were something new in the human experience — the sound of killing. The tapes had transfixed everyone who had heard them that day at the trial of Brady and Hindley in Chester, and had left some weeping. Mounsey fetched me a transcript from the next room.

At first it's just pathetic. 'Don't undress me, will you?' By the end it's Hindley's voice we're listening to: 'Shut up,' she whispers urgently. 'Shut up.'

'Oh, please, help,' cries the child, in pain.

'Shut up,' comes the woman's hard, flat voice. The child screams and chokes. 'Shut up or I'll forget myself and hit you one.'

'Please, Mummy, please!' These are her last words.

The Mounsey living room in Preston, Lancashire, was silent for a moment. 'I think that was a horrendous thing,' said Margaret, 'the fact that a woman would entice a child and not protect her.'

Brady and Hindley escaped execution by only a few months. When they were found guilty at Chester Assizes in 1966 — he of three murders, she of two — capital punishment had just been abolished in the United Kingdom. (It's interesting to speculate whether it would have been abolished if the Moors murders had been discovered earlier.) Both were given life sentences. Brady faded from the headlines, and is locked up, now a hopeless mental case. Hindley has never been out of the headlines.

Lord Longford, the penal reformer whom the London tabloids delight in calling 'the potty peer,' has campaigned hard for her release and describes her as 'a very gentle person.' In 1987, perhaps in hopes of finally winning her freedom after twenty-one years behind bars, Hindley responded to an anguished letter from the mother of Keith Bennett, who went missing in 1964, admitting knowledge of his murder as well as that of Pauline Reade, sixteen when she disappeared July 12, 1963. Hindley was spirited to Saddleworth Moor by the police, and was able to point out the spot where Pauline Reade was buried. But Keith Bennett's body has yet to be found.

In another obvious attempt to create a new image for her with the public, in fall 1989 Longford and some of Hindley's supporters released to the media a photograph of her in academic gown after she had received an Open University degree she had earned while in prison. It did little good: the response in the media was generally negative.

Who was – is – Myra Hindley? The passing years make the question no easier to answer. Certainly she is no longer the brazen blonde who laughed and joked with Brady in the prisoners' dock and, in a flat, emotionless voice, denied any knowledge of the killings. On the contrary, a *Sunday Times* interviewer in 1982 found her a soft-spoken, warmly engaging woman with dark, close-cropped hair and arresting blue eyes, a woman who, in spite of having spent a quarter of a century behind bars, is very much up with social issues and trends. She had been helped, she told the interviewer, by 'the love of my friends and my love of life. I have a lot of friends.' Sometimes though, she said, 'I feel I just want to lie down and die. I know I am hated, but for every thousand who hate me, there is one who loves me.'

She speaks the truth. A remarkable coterie of people – public figures, prison psychologists, lawyers, doctors and even a prison governor – have fallen under her thrall, sometimes to their later regret. In 1972, the governor of Holloway Prison, where Hindley was held at the time, was rebuked in Parliament for taking Hindley for a walk on Hampstead Heath.

Hindley's memories of that day, she related to the *Sunday Times*: 'The minute I stepped outside those gates, it was as though I had never been inside. Everything came back to me. It was the smells – of grass and trees, and throwing a ball for the governor's dog. There were children playing.'

A year later, Pat Cairns, a former nun who had become a prison officer, was given a six-year sentence for helping Hindley in a futile and ill-conceived escape attempt.

But others still believe in her. A Quaker welfare worker sends her flowers twice a month; a prison psychologist keeps a woolly toy Hindley gave her on her dressing table. Her friends speak of her intelligence, the ability she has to make each of them feel important in her life – as no doubt they are. And only when pressed will they admit that the one small reservation they still have about her is that, as she did in the beginning, she still denies having any hand in the murder of the young people, blaming it all on Brady.

139

On Saddleworth Moor, a raw February afternoon was drawing to a close. The last of the families out for a Sunday drive had departed. I scrambled up on the rocks that had pointed Joe Mounsey to the body of John Kilbride and looked down at the bleak and tortured landscape. Was Myra Hindley, then a chameleon, taking on the ideas, the lives of those around her, as her own, now a bleached zombie who took part in acts unspeakable, now the warm-hearted university graduate, all empathy and sensitivity? And, the most troubling question, how many of us, given the same conditioning, could become Myra Hindleys?

Back in Preston, Joe Mounsey had been at a loss for answers to these questions. 'She was more than a willing pupil of Brady,' he said, shaking his head in consternation. 'Maybe there are words to explain it all . . . Or maybe' – he walked to the window and looked out – 'maybe it's just the evidence of human inconsistency, that we are all different.'

Coming down the slope again from the top of the moor, leaping from rock to rock, sliding on the black peat, I could feel only gratitude that human inconsistency throws up more Joe Mounseys than Myra Hindleys.

SILK PYJAMAS FOR
THE CHAUFFEUR

At this point in our journey we start climbing again toward the daylight. Until now, we've been dealing with women murderers for whom there was little excuse. They killed in anger; frequently they killed with cunning. And sometimes they even got away with it. From here on, though, I'm dealing with women who were not so much murderers as enmeshed in murder. Most of them were foolish rather than wicked, and in a surprising number of cases they found themselves charged with murder and, in one case even executed, more because of their wayward sexual behaviour than for any proof they had killed.

None, in my book, is more pathetic than Alma Rattenbury, who lies now in an unmarked grave in a Bournemouth cemetery, only a few feet from the husband she was accused of helping to murder.

Francis Rattenbury was a Klondike adventurer, a fashionable architect, and designer of one of the best-loved buildings in Canada, the Empress Hotel in Victoria. Alma was a piano prodigy, a war hero twice wounded

141

at the Front working as a medical aide in the First World War, recipient of the Croix de Guerre, and, in the 1930s, a well-known songwriter. But it all ended in scandal and death as a result of nothing more than a tragic misunderstanding.

Today in Bournemouth, a super-genteel English resort, the events of the trial, even though they took place more than fifty years ago, seem unbelievably fresh. Ten minutes' drive from the cemetery, the Villa Madeira, where the murder occurred, is almost unchanged from that day; Anna Landstein, eighty-three, who has lived in the house for thirty-five years, led me into the lounge where an armchair is still positioned in front of the French doors precisely where Francis Rattenbury was sitting when he was struck down. The odd-looking pillared bungalow occupied by George Stoner, the then-eighteen-year-old chauffeur who was Alma's lover, is another ten minutes away by car.

Perhaps Alma and Francis were attracted to each other originally because they both had such an appetite for life. Rattenbury, Yorkshire-born, was only newly arrived in British Columbia when he won the competition to design the gingerbread legislative buildings that still bring a touch of the fantastic to the waterfront in Victoria, the provincial capital. Rattenbury was a restless personality who could never stick to one thing for long, and when gold was discovered in the Klondike in northern Canada, he established a supply company, had steamers built, and became a big name on the frontier. When he married Eleanor Nunn in 1898, he took her, in typical Teddy Roosevelt-roughrider style, over the rugged Whitehorse

142

Pass, and they spent their honeymoon cruising Lake Bennett on one of his steamers.

Over the years, though, as Rattenbury traced some of the choicest architectural assignments in the opening West — including the Empress Hotel where English-style afternoon tea is still a tradition — his frantic bursts of energy alternated with curious bouts of lassitude. By 1922, when he was fifty-five, his image was at an end, and he was feeling like an old man. Then, Alma Pakenham, slender, beautiful, vivacious and already twice married, came into his life, and Francis Rattenbury rediscovered his youth.

Alma's beginnings were a mystery. Born in British Columbia, in obscure circumstances, of an English mother and, possibly, a German prospector father, she was described by one of her early teachers as 'a brilliantly clever child.' Musically gifted, at seventeen she appeared as a soloist with the Toronto Symphony Orchestra, playing both the piano and the violin in the same program.

In 1913, Alma married Caledon Dolling, a member of a prominent Ulster Catholic family, and when he joined up at the outbreak of the First World War, she followed him to England and got herself a job at the War Office. Dolling was killed by a shell in 1916 and, to bury her grief, Alma signed up with the Scottish Women's Hospital, working as an orderly and stretcher bearer, sometimes bringing in the wounded under fire.

When the guns were finally silenced, Alma, her sense of purpose gone, became one of those brittle, drifting flappers of the postwar years, briefly marrying Compton Pakenham, a former Coldstream Guards officer, with

143

whom she had a son, Christopher, and then leaving her incorrigibly idle husband to return to her mother in British Columbia.

Meeting her for the first time there, Rattenbury was enraptured. 'Butterflies eat out of her hands,' he wrote to his sister, later describing Alma as looking like 'a fragile Madonna.' His first wife, though, would not budge from their grand house on Oak Bay until he cut off the power, removed the furniture and finally made a cash settlement and agreed to build her another house. To Alma's intense displeasure, she had it built on a plot overlooking her old home.

But nothing could really spoil their early years of bliss. 'Ratz,' as Alma called her husband, built her a music room, and on December 27, 1928, a son, John, was born to them. The trouble was that starchy Victoria socialites, who had sided with Rattenbury's first wife in the bitter marital breakup, weren't prepared to accept his new wife, even denying her membership in the Victoria Musical Society. Rattenbury, too, quarrelled with members of his profession, and in 1929, after he had lost a good part of his fortune in that disastrous year, the couple resolved to move to England and make a new start.

They settled in Bournemouth – as close to a carbon copy of Victoria as you could find – and moved into Villa Madeira, a modest house with the advantage of being only a few minutes' walk from the seashore. The interior was as awkward as the outside was undistinguished, but it suited their purposes. On the ground floor, alongside the sitting room that opened through French doors into the garden, was a bedroom

144

and bathroom, which Rattenbury, considerably slowed by age now, enamoured of the bottle and no longer interested in sex, commandeered for himself, while Alma slept in an upstairs room she shared with John.

Soon, though, the unpredictable Ratz found new zest in promoting Alma's musical career. She had dabbled in song-writing in the past. Now he did everything in his power – contacting music publishers, making trips to London – to win acceptance for her songs. Soon their efforts were attended by success. They met famous people like Ambrose, the orchestra leader, and tenor Richard Tauber visited the Villa Madeira; published under the name 'Lozanne' Alma's tunes such as 'Dark-haired Marie,' sung by Peter Dawson, became hits.

And then, Ratz, always fierce in his enthusiasms, lost interest in her music and turned his attention to a local apartment development project. Increasingly deaf, his faculties sometimes impaired by alcohol, Rattenbury decided he no longer wanted to drive. In September 1934, George Percy Stoner, eighteen but claiming to be twenty-two, answered their advertisement in the local paper for a chauffeur-handyman. Soon Stoner moved into the front upstairs bedroom, next to that of Irene Riggs, the maid-companion the Rattenburys had hired earlier. And the scene was set for tragedy.

F. Tennyson Jesse, one of Britain's pre-eminent writers on criminal matters, who attended the Rattenbury trial, wrote in the introduction to the official trial transcript: 'Mrs. Rattenbury was a highly sexed woman and six years of being deprived of sexual satisfaction had combined with tuberculosis, from which she suffered, to bring her to the edge of nymphomania.' Whether we accept Jesse's diagnosis, the fact was that Alma quickly became infatuated with Stoner and, while her husband slept in his bedroom downstairs, she brought the young chauffeur into the large main bedroom where she slept with the infant John.

By the following March, Alma was making up a story for Ratz about having to go to London for a minor operation in connection with her tuberculosis. Stoner accompanied her; they stayed in adjoining rooms at the Royal Palace Hotel in Kensington, and she took him on a shopping spree at Harrods, buying him silk pyjamas, a grey suit, and shoes and shirts. They lingered three days in town, walking, attending the theatre and cinema, then returned to Bournemouth around 10:30 p.m. on March 22. As she kissed him goodnight, Ratz, who had been drinking, asked her no questions.

Two days later though, Rattenbury was feeling depressed. Not even a drive, with Stoner behind the wheel, to see a litter of puppies cheered him up, and after tea he read aloud portions of a dreary novel in which the aging hero contemplates suicide. 'You could admire a person doing away with himself because he was old and doddering,' said Ratz as he closed the book.

Trying to think of some way to cheer him up, Alma phoned a business associate of Ratz's in nearby Bridport and arranged that she and Ratz would visit him the following day to discuss financial details concerning the apartment project in which the two men were involved. They would stay overnight.

At 9:30 that evening, after a game of cards, she kissed

her husband goodnight and left him sitting in the chair in front of the French doors. Forty-five minutes later, returning from her Sunday off, Irene Riggs let herself in through the front door. On the way to get herself something to eat in the kitchen, she heard heavy breathing. She knocked on the door of Rattenbury's bedroom, went in and found it empty. Then, oddly, she went up to bed without checking the sitting room.

Going to the bathroom a few minutes later, she saw Stoner leaning over the banister at the top of the stairs. 'Just checking to see if the lights are off,' he said, before returning to his room. Alma, who had made Irene her confidante, joined her in her room a few moments later, and they chatted amiably about the plan to take Ratz to Bridport the following day.

Shortly afterwards, Irene heard a scream from downstairs. Running down, she found Alma in the sitting room with Rattenbury who was slouched back in his chair, his eye blackened, his head a mass of blood. 'Someone has hurt Ratz,' Alma cried. 'Telephone the doctor!' Her wartime training served her well. While Irene phoned, she ran to the bathroom, fetched a towel and wrapped it around her husband's head to staunch the bleeding. Then, as she tried to undress Rattenbury, she sent Stoner in the car to fetch the doctor.

At that point Alma did something desperately foolish. She drank a stiff shot of whisky, threw up, then drank some more. By the time Dr. William O'Donnell arrived and ordered that Rattenbury be removed to a nursing home where he could get proper treatment, Alma was potted. When Constable Arthur Bagwell arrived at the

147

door at 2:00 a.m. to investigate, she tried to dance with him and kiss him, and declared, 'I know who did it. I did it! With a mallet!'

When Dr. O'Donnell returned to the house at 4:00 a.m. after doing what he could for Rattenbury, he found police questioning the very intoxicated Alma. Taking her by the arm, he marched her firmly upstairs to her room, gave her half a grain of morphine and saw she went to bed. Two hours later, still incoherent, she was wakened on police orders and brought staggering downstairs. 'Tell Stoner he must give me the mallet,' she whispered to Irene as they took her away to the police station.

Yes, she told them at the station, she had hit her husband over the head with a mallet after he had dared her to kill him while they were playing cards. Charged, she responded, 'That's right, I did it deliberately, and I would do it again.'

Her efforts to protect her lover were in vain. Rattenbury died three days later, and Stoner, along with Alma, was charged with murder. While in custody, he told a constable, 'I watched through the French windows and saw her kiss him goodnight, then leave the room. I waited and crept in through the French window, which was unlocked.' He added: 'You know, there should be a doctor with her when they tell her I am arrested because she will go out of her mind.'

He was not far wrong. Alma tortured herself with guilt. 'The truth is,' she told the prison governor, 'it is my fault, absolutely.' When Frank Titterton, one of the singers whose recordings had brought 'Lozanne' fame, visited her in Holloway Prison, he found her wan and worrying about her children – Christopher, who was now thirteen, and John, six. 'Oh, I am so hungry for some music,' she told him as he stood to go. He leaned forward and softly sang in her ear one of her best-known songs. She went into ecstasies, he wrote later.

In prison she wrote a song for George Stoner that began, 'By some mistake my spirit held you dear, but now I wake in agony and fear.' Her letters to her children were decorated with musical notes and often ended with little tunes.

It was her closeness to her children, in fact, that finally brought her to see that nothing would be gained by persisting with her story that she had killed Ratz. In all likelihood, she could not save Stoner, and if she too was imprisoned or executed, her children would be motherless.

Some of the biggest rogues in British penal history – poisoners, child murderers and men who chopped their wives into little bits – have stood in the dock of Number One Court at the Old Bailey. But it's probably fair to say that when Alma Rattenbury, still slim and looking younger than her reputed thirty-eight years, took her place in the dock beside the pale and surprisingly gentle-looking Stoner, she was among the most publicly reviled prisoners ever to stand on that spot. Wrote Jesse: 'There was probably no one in England, and no one in court when the trial opened, save Mrs. Rattenbury, her solicitor and counsel, and Miss Riggs, who did not think Mrs. Rattenbury was guilty of the crime of murder.' Attending the trial, Jesse was accompanied by the well-known actor Raymond Massey, who, long ago in Toronto, had attended kindergarten with Alma.

In the box, wrote Jesse, 'she was an excellent witness. Her voice was low and rich. She gave a great impression of truthfulness, and she was astonishingly well-controlled. Only a nervous tic in the side of her face, which jerked perpetually, betrayed the tension of her mind.'

The evening her husband was attacked, she testified, Stoner had been angry about them going on the trip to Bridport the following day. He didn't like the prospect of Alma sharing a room with her husband. 'He was very jealous of Mr. Rattenbury,' she said in reply to a question. 'Unnecessarily so.'

Later, she reported, after her talk with Irene, Stoner joined her in her room. He seemed agitated and, when she asked the reason, 'he told me that I was not going to Bridport the next day as he had hurt Ratz. It did not penetrate my head what he did say to me at all until I heard Ratz groan, and then my brain became alive and I jumped out of bed.' Stoner told her he had hit Rattenbury over the head with a mallet that he had hidden in the garden.

The testimony that certainly did Alma most harm with the public concerned her making love with Stoner in the bedroom where John was sleeping. 'Did you really choose the room where the child was asleep?' she was asked. She seemed surprised by the question. 'Why not? The little boy was asleep. He was a sound sleeper . . . I did not consider that dreadful.'

'You cannot have any feeling but disgust for her,' Justice Christmas Humphreys told the jury. She was, he said, 'a woman so lost to all decency, so entirely without any moral sense that she would stop at nothing to gain

150

her ends.' And then we can almost imagine the wink as he told the members of the jury that they should not, of course, convict her simply because she was 'an adulteress of the most unpleasant type.' After going over the details of what he called the 'orgy' in London, the judge left no doubt that he believed there had been a conspiracy to murder Rattenbury: 'Do you believe that while they were in London the future was not discussed? Would not something have to be done with, or to, Rattenbury?'

As Jesse points out, the judge's prejudiced remarks were based on the odd assumption that Alma, a woman of the world with two children and married to an acquiescent and undemanding husband, would think of disposing of him so that she could marry the chauffeur, who she now knew to be eighteen.

Turning to Stoner, Mr. Justice Humphreys cast further guilt on Alma by declaring, 'Whatever your verdict may be in this case, his position is due to the domination of that woman over him.'

By Friday, the last day of the five-day trial, Stoner, who had not given evidence, still sat apparently unmoved, his eyes downcast. But Alma Rattenbury, observed Jesse, 'looked twenty years older than she had on Monday. On the last day even her hands changed colour, and were a livid, greenish white.'

The jury returned its verdicts with merciful speed: Alma Victoria Rattenbury – not guilty; George Percy Stoner – guilty.

'Oh, no!' cried Alma, stepping forward as if there had been some mistake. Two wardresses grabbed her and helped her from the dock as the judge put on his black hat and prepared to sentence Stoner to death. Alma was free — but her freedom was of no use to her. She was booed by the crowd waiting outside the Old Bailey, but it all made no difference to her. Stoner, the man she loved, would hang, and if she lived to be a hundred she would still regard herself as being responsible for his death, as well as that of her husband.

Four days after the trial ended, a cowman, William Mitchell, saw a woman sitting on the bank of a river near Christchurch, just outside Bournemouth. She was writing when he first saw her, but when he looked in that direction again she was walking toward the river. He thought she was going to pick flowers, but then he noticed she had a knife in her hand. At the water's edge she crouched, then toppled in. Mitchell ran to the bank and waded in, but she was already beyond his reach. 'All this time she was staring fixedly at me with a terrible look in her eyes,' he would say. He threw her coat to her from the riverbank, yelling, 'Catch hold of this.' But, as he did so, her head went back and blood oozed to the surface from a wound in her chest. 'She turned her head and looked at me and uttered one long cry which sounded like "O-o-h!" '

In her suicide note Alma had written, 'Eight o'clock, and after so much walking I have got here. Oh, to see the swans and the spring flowers and to smell them . . . It was not intentional, my coming here. I tossed a coin, like Stoner always did, and it came down "Christchurch." It is beautiful here. What a lovely world, really . . . pray God nothing stops me tonight.' She had tried that morning to throw herself under a subway train at Oxford

Circus and later under a bus, but in both cases there had been too many people around. 'It is beautiful here and I am alone,' she concluded. 'Thank God for peace at last. God bless my children and look after them.'

After 300,000 people signed a petition for clemency, George Stoner was reprieved. He served seven years in prison and was released to join the armed forces during the Second World War. He took part in the Normandy landings. He lives quietly with his wife in their Bournemouth bungalow, and was never again in trouble with the law until, in 1990, at the age of seventy-four, he admitted in magistrates court assaulting a twelve-year-old boy in a public lavatory near his home. He was put on probation for two years.

'He never struck me as that kind of chap,' commented Bournemouth's retired former deputy chief constable, George Gates, eighty-three, who arrested Stoner in 1935. 'He was reserved and introspective.'

Walking through the Villa Madeira with Mrs. Landstein, it seemed that little had changed. If Alma came laughing gaily through the French doors from the garden, the only thing she'd notice missing is the grand piano she brought with her from Victoria. When Mrs. Landstein and her husband came here from Austria and bought the house, they had no idea of its associations – until an electrician, fixing the wiring, joked, 'Do you want me to mop up the blood?' The murder never troubled Mrs. Landstein, whose husband died several years ago, until, following the airing of a television drama about the case, someone threw a brick through the leaded front windows.

Bournemouth though, like Victoria, does not seem to

153

have taken to Alma. To those who knew her, she was a kind, affectionate and talented woman who was guilty, certainly, of bad judgment. But, said Mrs. Landstein in a recent letter to me, after living in Bournemouth for thirty-five years they say of her, 'just as they say of poor Alma: "She was a foreigner, you know." '

THE
UNFORGIVABLE SIN

Aigburth (pronounced 'Egg-birth') is not the sort of place most people imagine when they hear Liverpool mentioned. Forget about gutted, graffiti-scarred public-housing estates, deserted docks and the race riots of the 1980s. Think instead of a pleasant suburb running down to the green banks of the River Mersey.

But it's still a long way from Alabama, and when cotton broker James Maybrick brought his bride, Florence, here from Mobile in the early 1880s, it must have seemed a damp and chilly spot, and the people her husband introduced her to a hard-nosed and dour lot compared with the gentler society of the American South.

Battlecrease House, the slightly forbidding mansion where she experienced so much unhappiness, still stands across from the rococo architecture of the Liverpool Cricket Club (1841) and it's easy to imagine Florence, fashionably plump, with baby-doll blue eyes and naturally blonde hair tinged with red, and dressed in the latest London creation, walking restlessly among the laburnums as if the garden was a prison yard. In marrying Maybrick,

155

twenty-three years her senior, she made a mistake; like Alma Rattenbury she thought a sexual adventure would provide some sort of escape; and, at the conclusion of what Judge Gerald Sparrow has called, 'perhaps the most astounding murder trial of the nineteenth century,' she too paid a price out of all proportion to her offence.

Cotton, of course, was the link that joined Liverpool with Mobile, Alabama. Florence, born in 1862, was the second child of William Chandler, a cotton merchant (and niece of John Campbell, secretary of war in the Southern Confederacy), and cotton was what brought Jim Maybrick to America. As it happens, she met him, not under the magnolias, but on the White Star liner *Baltic* on one of those transatlantic voyages on which, if an attractive young woman didn't get at least three proposals of marriage, she counted it a wasted trip. Florence, who was only eighteen, was accompanied, of course, by her mother.

Her mother! When you know about Florence's mother, you begin to understand a lot of what happened later. She was one of those bold American women of the late-Victorian era who saw marriage as the road to fortune and, perhaps, a European title, and who didn't allow themselves to become discouraged by early failures. When Florence's father died the year after she was born, her mother soon married a Confederate officer, who also died shortly after − of tuberculosis. She passed the remainder of the war sensibly in Paris with her two children, returning afterwards to New York to stay with her cousin, the second Mrs. Cornelius Vanderbilt. Back in Paris a few years later, she married Baron Adolph von Roques, a Prussian cavalry officer whose taste for big spending and high living matched her own.

Florence would write later that she got her education in Europe and America from tutors and governesses, but her education in real-life values came firsthand from her mother. She learned to perfection the role of Woman as Ornament, graduating with honours in Winning Power through Men, and she showed impressive mastery of such skills as shopping for designer clothes and the effortless spending of significant sums of money. To say that the teenage Florence Chandler was, when Jim Maybrick met her, a brainless little ninny would be unkind, but even her mother admitted, 'My daughter is not a woman of great penetration.'

The blunt truth is that Florence, with her innocent, deep-blue, almost violet eyes, was a pawn in a game for grown-ups: to a man of Maybrick's age, a voluptuous and slightly exotic American child-bride would be a choice piece of fancy goods to bring home to Liverpool; to Florence's mother, whose finances were in rocky shape, a wealthy son-in-law was the means of her financial salvation. Florence's prospects as a potential heiress back home in Mobile were discreetly talked up, while Jim spoke grandly of his expanding business horizons. But when they were married at fashionable St. James, Piccadilly, in London, on July 27, 1881, the best Maybrick could come up with as a marriage settlement was a £2,000 life-insurance policy, and all Florence had to contribute was a mortgage that yielded her a £125 a year.

But, in Norfolk, Virginia, where they lived intermittently in the first years of their marriage, and later

157

in Liverpool, Maybrick concealed from his wife just how badly his business was doing, and they lived in style. At Battlecrease House, where they eventually settled, a staff of five servants was needed to run the twenty-room, sumptuously furnished house, a staff that Florence as a young wife, and an American at that, could not bring herself to order about.

On the surface at least, their lives together followed the accepted pattern. A boy, James Chandler, was born to them in America in 1882; a girl, Gladys Evelyn, in England in 1886. They enjoyed going out to dances, dinner parties, card parties and horse meets, and counted it a slack week if they were home alone more than one or two evenings. He called her 'Bunny,' and, according to a visitor to their home at that time, they would often walk the grounds of Battlecrease House arm in arm, and she would sit on his lap and tell him how many grey hairs he was getting.

What people around Florence didn't notice at the time — what she herself didn't know until it was too late — was that she was friendless. If she'd been older, maybe more personable, not even the fact that she was not English would have isolated her. But, without her mother (who was living in Paris now, and receiving a small income from Maybrick) and her family around her, and living in a strange country, Florence Maybrick was dangerously exposed.

It first came home when, in 1887, her husband finally revealed to her that his assets amounted to only £1,500 and that they were in serious financial difficulties. He reduced her housekeeping allowance to a miserable £7 a week, out of which she was expected to budget for food as well as pay the servants. Her alarm was only compounded by the secret knowledge that she had been borrowing to buy clothes and put bets on horses and owed £600.

'Is life worth living?' she wrote to her mother, the only person she could turn to. 'I would gladly give up the house tomorrow and move somewhere else, but Jim says it would ruin him outright. For one must keep up appearances otherwise all claims would pour in at once and how could Jim settle with what he has now?'

And James Maybrick, who had once seemed so solid, so respectable, so Victorian, was turning out to be a sham in other ways. A pathetic hypochondriac, he was forever dosing himself with patent medicines. Ever since he had come down with malaria in Norfolk, Virginia, in 1877, and had been treated successfully with arsenic and strychnine, he had been taking poisons on a daily basis – a not uncommon practice in the nineteenth century. Florence was so worried that he was damaging his health that she mentioned it both to his doctor and hers, but when she remonstrated with her husband, he told her to mind her own business.

The news that finally and totally shattered Florence's peace of mind was that Maybrick had had a mistress for years, a former jewellery clerk by whom he had five children, and whom he was still seeing. He was also paying her £100 a year. It was the moment above all others when a woman needs a friend in whom to confide. A friend would have urged patience, discretion, and might have pointed out that Maybrick's precarious finances could

159

hardly have been adequate to support three households, eliminating divorce as an option. Above all, a friend, one accustomed to the moral climate, would have advised Florence against the reckless course upon which she set herself: revenge.

She began flirting recklessly with Maybrick's brother, Edwin, telling him one night at table, loudly enough for Jim at the other end to hear, 'If I had met you first, things might have been different.' James Maybrick, according to a witness, dropped his knife, glared down the table and flushed deep red before recovering his composure. Love letters, too, were reportedly found in her bureau to a lawyer friend in London.

It was when Alfred Brierley, six feet tall, handsome and sporting a dashing pointed beard, came to a dance at Battlecrease House that Florence lost all sense. Brierley, like her husband, was a cotton broker, though fifteen years younger than Maybrick and a bachelor, and she set her heart on winning him. In March 1889, it was she who taunted Brierley with being afraid to meet her, she who arranged a rendezvous in London with him, she who telegraphed Flatman's, a hotel in Covent Garden commonly used by Liverpool cotton brokers, and reserved a two-room suite for them in the name of 'Mr. and Mrs. Thomas Maybrick, of Manchester' (Thomas was one of James's four brothers) and told her husband she was visiting a sick aunt.

The only explanation that does Florence any credit at all is that she was going out of her way to provide her husband with the evidence for a divorce. Otherwise, she was either acting out of sheer unthinking stupidity or

striking out blindly in an effort to hurt him publicly.
Brierley, flattered initially by the attentions of the pretty
Mrs. Maybrick, must soon have recognized that he was
being used by her. Although a waiter at Flatman's would
report seeing him there for the full three days of Mrs.
Maybrick's visit, sometimes having breakfast with her,
another report has him encountering business friends from
Liverpool at the hotel, and shamefacedly sneaking away
after the first night. Florence herself explained later to
her lawyer: 'Before we parted he gave me to understand
that he cared for somebody else and could not marry me,
and that rather than face the disgrace of discovery he
would blow his brains out.' At any rate, Brierley very soon
after booked himself on a two-month cruise to the
Mediterranean, apparently to put an end to the affair.
And there the undignified episode would likely have ended
– if James Maybrick had not died two months later.

At Battlecrease House, the Maybricks had not been
sleeping together, and their rows were frequent. On March
29, the day after Florence returned from her London
rendezvous, Alfred Brierley was with the Maybricks in
a group that went to the Grand National, the highlight
of the steeplechase season, run at Aintree, near Liverpool.
Maybrick was outraged when Florence, ignoring his
orders, walked back to the stands alone with Brierley,
and when they got home he blacked her eye and tore her
dress, yelling, 'This scandal will be all over town
tomorrow.' He told the housemaid, Bessie Brierley (as
far as we know, no relation), to call Mrs. Maybrick a cab
and turn her out of the house.

Elizabeth Humphreys, the cook and about the only

friend Florence had in the house, would say that Maybrick 'raved and stamped like a madman.' When his wife was making to leave, he ordered her to take off her fur cape, which he had bought her to go up to London. Humphreys told him, 'Don't send the mistress away tonight. Where can she go? Let her stay until morning.' After some more shouting, she reported, he slumped across a bench in the hall, and the servants hurried Florence upstairs to bed.

Next morning, Florence made the mistake of taking her troubles to Mrs. Briggs, a neighbour who was divorced and who, she thought, was her friend. Mrs. Briggs was all understanding, took her to see her own solicitor, who was used to handling separation agreements, then took her to see the family physician, Dr. Hopper. Surprisingly, Dr. Hopper went up to Battlecrease House and effected a reconciliation between the warring couple, even getting Maybrick to agree to pay his wife's debts.

The trouble was only starting. Some time in the following month Brierley, the maid, and Alice Yapp, the nanny, saw Florence soaking some flypapers in a bowl in her bedroom. The flypapers had been purchased at Wokes's, a nearby druggists,' and she made no attempt to conceal what she was doing. At her trial, Florence would say that, for many years, she had used a facewash 'prescribed by Dr. Greggs of Brooklyn' consisting of arsenic and elderflower water, among other things. She had lost the prescription, and, with a ball coming up on April 30 and an eruption spoiling her complexion, she was making up her own approximation of it, soaking the flypapers to obtain arsenic. On April 27, James Maybrick complained of a numbness in his legs and vomiting, symptoms he had also experienced earlier in the month on a trip to London (when he settled Florence's debts), but he still insisted on riding to the Wirral Races, where he was soaked in a downpour of rain. He arrived home late, after dining with friends across the Mersey in Cheshire, and by next morning he was feeling very ill. Dr. Richard Humphreys was sent for. On an earlier visit, Florence had told the doctor she was worried because her husband was taking a white powder that might be harming him. 'Well,' replied the doctor lightly, 'if he should ever die suddenly, call me and I can say we had some conversation about it.' On April 27, Florence again expressed her concern to the doctor, but when Humphreys questioned his patient about it, Maybrick denied taking strychnine or arsenic.

On Monday, April 29, Florence purchased another two dozen flypapers. The following day, by which Maybrick was well enough to go to his office, Florence, her complexion apparently repaired to her satisfaction, attended a masked ball, escorted by Edwin Maybrick.

Poison was the method of choice for most women murderers in the last century simply because, as the sick-nurses and frequently the cook ministering to their husband's needs, they had every opportunity to administer the poison. But Florence Maybrick had almost nothing to do with preparing food for her husband. The busybody Mrs. Briggs was now taking her meals with the Maybricks and even ordering what should be cooked. On May 1, Florence wrapped up a jug of a patent food preparation for Maybrick to take to the office. Captain Irving, a friend of Maybrick's who was away at sea by the time his friend

163

had died and his wife was on trial for murder, would say later that, after drinking the patent food in his office that day, Maybrick complained of feeling unwell. But he took a packet from his pocket, added the contents to a glass of water, drank it off and declared shortly after that he felt much better. Irving was not surprised: 'Everybody knew Jim was always taking some medicine or other. Why, his office was more like a chemist's shop than anything else. You saw almost nothing else but medicine bottles. It was well known,' he added, 'that James Maybrick had been in the habit of taking strychnine for years.'

On May 3, Dr. Humphreys received an urgent call from Florence at midnight; her husband, she said, was very ill and experiencing 'a gnawing pain from the hips down to the knees.' For several days Maybrick's health fluctuated as he experienced bouts of vomiting and diarrhoea.

At this point, Florence, with her special gift for disaster, wrote a letter to Brierley. 'Dearest,' it began, and went on to say: 'Since my return I have been nursing M day and night. He is sick unto death.' Many Americans would come forward later to say the expression 'sick unto death' was commonly used in the South to mean, very sick. The English interpreted it to mean that Maybrick was about to die.

That the letter came to public attention at all owes much to Florence's naivety. She sealed it up and ran out to the gate where the nanny, Alice Yapp, was playing with the children. 'Will you post this for me, please?' she said, handing it to the girl. The appropriately named Yapp had been leading the below-stairs gossip about Florence and the mysterious flypapers. Her story in court was that, on the way to the post office, little Gladys, age three, dropped the envelope in the mud and stained it. Yapp opened it, meaning to put the letter in a fresh envelope, and her eye fell on the contents. ('Did it not occur to you,' she was asked in the witness box, 'that you could get a clean envelope and put it unopened into that?' 'Oh, I never thought of that!' she replied.)

Yapp, whose explanation drew clucks of disbelief from Florence's supporters in the courtroom, knew exactly what to do with the letter. She took it to Edwin Maybrick and the neighbour, Mrs. Briggs, who were both in regular attendance on the sick Maybrick. Mrs. Briggs's surprise at reading the contents stretches belief: she would admit later that it was she who had suggested Florence write to Brierley. In London shortly afterwards, another Maybrick brother, Michael, a composer who, under the name Stephen Adams, produced such Victorian favourites as 'The Holy City' and 'Star of Bethlehem,' received a telegram from Mrs. Briggs, which, for its wording, deserves a place in the melodrama Hall of Fame. It said: 'Come at once; strange things going on here.'

With suspicion being voiced openly that Maybrick had been poisoned, Florence was effectively dethroned as mistress of the house, while Alice Yapp and several of the servants joined with Mrs. Briggs and the brothers in the delicious intrigue of spying on her at all hours. Already, medicines and food items were being removed from the sick room for analysis, and interest would focus on a bottle of Valentine's Meat Juice, which proved to

165

contain half a grain of arsenic. Florence's explanation in court was that, on the evening of May 9, she was sitting with Jim when he implored her to give him some of his famous 'white powder,' but she refused. 'I was overwrought, terribly anxious, miserably unhappy, and his evident distress utterly unnerved me. He told me the powder would not harm him. I then consented.' But by the time she returned with 'the bottle' (apparently, the meat juice bottle), he was asleep, and she left it on a side table without giving him any.

The same evening a nurse would report hearing Maybrick say repeatedly to his wife, 'Oh, Bunny, Bunny, how could you do it? I did not think it of you.' The words would sound incriminating in the light of the murder charge against Florence; in fact, Maybrick was probably referring to her unfaithfulness.

Two days later, little hope was being held out for James Maybrick; around mid-morning Florence fell into a coma, apparently brought on by nervous strain, was carried to her room and did not recover consciousness for twenty-four hours. She was unaware that, at 8:40 p.m., her husband had died and that immediately Mrs. Briggs, Alice Yapp and the brothers had ransacked the house, looking for suspicious substances. They did not have far to look. In cupboards, in drawers, in hat boxes, in every possible place, they found bottles containing enough arsenic, it turned out, to kill fifty people. One of the doctors had prescribed a preparation called Fowler's Solution, an arsenic preparation, during the final illness; also, arsenic was found in the remains of the food formula Maybrick had taken with him to the office.

166

On May 14, Florence was still prostrate in bed when police Superintendent Isaac Bryning was shown into her bedroom. 'Mrs. Maybrick,' he announced, 'I am about to say something to you. After I have said what I intend to say, if you reply, be careful how you do reply, because whatever you say may be used in evidence against you. Mrs. Maybrick, you are in custody on suspicion of causing the death of your late husband, James Maybrick, on the 11th instant.'

She made no reply. Lying in bed in the days that followed, watched over night and day by policemen and hostile nurses, Florence Maybrick must have endured a level of loneliness few people have had to face. After three days, her mother, the baroness, arrived in Liverpool with all the majesty of an ocean liner sailing up the Mersey. 'How could you have delivered her up to the police in this way and not a friend by her?' she demanded of Michael Maybrick.

'I assure you we had no idea matters would result in this way,' he replied weakly.

'But the children, how could you ruin their future? You are doing her to death among you, and for what motive?'

'I would never have believed anything wrong of her,' said Maybrick, 'I would have stood by her, and I did – until the letter to a man was found.' What man? Why, Brierley, the man she had met at some dances the past winter. 'I wish I could meet Brierley,' he ended lamely.

'Yes,' exclaimed the baroness, 'in my country and among the men I have known, they would have met Brierley instead of calling in the police!' And who, she

167

demanded with penetrating eye, had found the letter?
'You?'

'Nurse,' he replied.

'If she found it, why did she not give it back to her
mistress?' There is only one word for the baroness's
performance: magnificent.

Ignoring protesting policemen and interfering nurses,
she then barged into her daughter's room, demanding to
know what was gong on. 'They think I have poisoned
Jim,' said Florence faintly.

'Poisoned Jim! Why, if he is poisoned, he poisoned
himself. He made a positive apothecary's shop of himself,
as we all know.'

The baroness, we are pleased to learn, went to the
nursery and told Alice Yapp to her face, 'You are an
ungrateful, disloyal servant,' and later had to be locked
in her room to prevent her interfering when her daughter
was removed by cab to Walton Jail.

The results of the autopsy, revealed at the inquest on
June 6, were a great disappointment to the Florence
Maybrick hanging party. Only about one-tenth of a grain
of arsenic was found in the organs of James Maybrick
(two grains is reckoned to be a fatal dose). The medical
evidence at the trial, which began in St. George's Hall,
Liverpool, on July 31, 1889, was so conflicting as to be
virtually meaningless. It was not clear whether Maybrick
had died from arsenic, strychnine or, indeed, from poison
at all.

Evidence given at the trial shows that arsenic was used
by those under pressure then much as cocaine is today.
A druggist testified that Maybrick would stop by his store

as often as five times a day for an arsenic-based 'pick-me-up,' and had increased his habit to the point where he was taking a third of a grain a day. But that was not so unusual: as many as sixteen gentlemen from the cotton exchange would arrive every morning for their arsenic tonics, which were also believed to spur sexual appetite. Valentine Blake, the son of an Irish Member of Parliament, would reveal four years after the trial that he had given Maybrick a significant amount of arsenic as part of a business transaction three months before the cotton broker died.

But the issue wasn't really arsenic: it was adultery. In the stifling moral atmosphere of the time, it was thought a woman capable of adultery was capable of anything, and Florence was clearly an adulteress. Under the law at that time she did not have the right to go into the witness box to defend herself, but, with the permission of the judge, she was allowed to make a statement. In the end, it only harmed her cause. After trying to explain about the flypapers and her adding arsenic to the meat juice, she concluded: 'For the love of my children, and for the sake of their future, a complete reconciliation had taken place between myself and my husband. The day before he died I made a full and free confession to him and received his entire forgiveness.'

Society was not so quick to forgive. Today, Florence's infidelity would be seen as a not-unusual consequence of marriage breakdown and, weighed against her husband's long-standing liaison, would probably count for little. In that day of the double standard, Maybrick's affair was barely mentioned at the trial, whereas even Florence's

169

defence counsel, Sir Charles Russell (later Lord Russell, the Lord Chief Justice), had to acknowledge that her adultery amounted to 'a grave moral guilt.' In attacking the double standard, he had this to say: 'In a man such faults are too often regarded with toleration, and they bring him often but a few penal consequences. But, in the case of a wife, in the case of a woman, it is with her sex the unforgivable sin.'

The judge, Sir James Fitzjames Stephen, was mentally confused and soon afterwards retired because of incapacity, but through his mental haze he had grasped one central idea: this was not simply a case where the jury must decide whether Maybrick had been poisoned. 'You must decide it as a great and highly important case . . . involving in itself a most highly important moral question. For a person,' said the judge in his confusing summing up, 'to go on deliberately administering poison to a poor, helpless, sick man upon whom she had already inflicted a dreadful injury − an injury fatal to married life − the person who could do such a thing as that must indeed be destitute of the least trace of human feeling.'

It took the jury only thirty-eight minutes to bring in a guilty verdict. After he imposed the death penalty, Judge Stephen was booed and hissed as he left St. George's Hall. It was said, not without truth, that the Maybrick affair was England's Dreyfus case; that just as the persecution of the young Jewish officer in France had aroused massive reaction, Florence's trial exposed the shortcomings of the British legal system and inspired mass meetings and half a million people to petition for her reprieve. Three days before the execution date, word arrived at Walton Jail that her sentence had been commuted to life imprisonment on the grounds that, although the evidence showed that Florence had attempted to kill her husband with arsenic, there was a reasonable doubt as to whether that was the actual cause of his death. In effect, she was being sentenced to life imprisonment for attempted murder.

Queen Victoria had been outraged by the Maybrick affair and had been loath to grant a reprieve. Now she insisted Florence Maybrick must not get an early release. As the plight of Florence Maybrick − now dutifully sewing five shirts a week and surviving on bread and gruel − received more and more attention in the United States, the British justice system came under increasing fire. There had been no criminal-appeal mechanism open to Florence Maybrick but, largely as a result of her case, the law was changed to permit appeals in criminal cases. But while she lived, none of Victoria's prime ministers had the temerity to suggest Florence's release. It was only in 1901, after the queen's death, that the government announced she would be released in three years. On January 25, 1904, at age forty-one, she emerged from prison, embittered, to be spirited across the Channel to France, with an escort provided by the American ambassador, and there reunited with her elderly mother. It must have been a touching scene.

Returning to the United States, Florence gave interviews, went on the lecture circuit and wrote her autobiography, *My Fifteen Lost Years*. But gradually she faded from public attention and died in squalor, surrounded by her cats in a small house near the village of South Kent, Connecticut, on October 23, 1941. She

171

was seventy-six, and her grave is marked by a wooden cross bearing her initials, F.E.C.M. (Florence Elizabeth Chandler Maybrick).

But the real Florence Chandler, the carefree young woman whose mother had taught her that life was a simple matter of pleasing men, and who had discovered otherwise, had died here at Battlecrease House long before that.

HIS DYING
WORDS

Sixty years on from the events at Battlecrease House and in a small Ontario town, attitudes toward sexual misconduct had not advanced in the least. As a consequence a couple would pay with their lives. It was Christmas 1946. On Main Street, beyond the prison wall, men on ladders were stringing up lights. This would be a special Christmas: the boys were home from the war at last. In Welland, half an hour's drive from Niagara Falls, the shops were filled with extravagant trifles that hadn't been seen since before the war, and among the womenfolk of those returned soldiers, it was an unlucky wife who couldn't strut and proclaim her pregnant condition.

Even the royal family in faraway London had found itself infected with the spirit of romance, and the newspapers were full of rumours about a possible wedding between King George VI's daughter, Princess Elizabeth, and the handsome young Prince Philip of Greece.

But, in the modest manse belonging to the United Church mission to − to use the quaint title of that day

173

– 'the non-Anglo Saxon people of Welland County,' the Reverend Dr. Harvey D. Forster and his wife, Olive, could take no share in the pleasures of the season. On that evening of December 5, Forster was on the telephone, making a last, desperate attempt to reach Canada's justice minister (and future prime minister) Louis St. Laurent, who was attending one of the early meetings of the just-founded United Nations in New York. He intended to make a final plea for clemency for another George and Elizabeth whose situation could not have been farther removed from that royal father and daughter in Buckingham Palace. In a few hours time, George and Elizabeth Popovich were due to be hanged in Welland County Jail for the murder of Louis Nato.

Even today, Thorald South, a rural municipality that skirts Welland, is no beauty spot, and in the 1930s and 1940s it was scrub poor and dotted with shanties where many immigrants from Eastern Europe got their start. Today, many of their children and grandchildren occupy important positions in Canada; then, the newcomers were looked down upon and referred to by people of British stock as 'Bohunks,' and, after the war, 'DPs' (Displaced Persons). Many worked at the Ontario Paper Company, a paper mill owned by the *Chicago Tribune*, while others earned an illicit living from bootlegging. Prominent locally in that business was Louis Nato, a stocky, barrel-chested guy of Italian origin who kept an ice-cream and candy store that operated irregularly and a back-door bootlegging business that was open all .hours. In the past Louis had operated his own taxi – a useful sideline for a bootlegger – and he still had the car he'd used, a magnificent 1932 seven-seater Pierce-Arrow.

In the early morning hours of June 17, 1946, one of Louis's neighbours, Helen Wizer, was wakened by a knocking at her door. She could be forgiven for believing what she saw on her doorstep was a ghost. It was the figure of a man, his head beaten and bloody, wearing a sweater but no trousers, and carrying a rope, which was still tied to his leg. Only after she had given him a glass of water did she recognize Louis. 'Him was swelled head,' she would say in court. 'He make me scare.'

When Louis discovered she had no phone, he went on to another neighbour, John 'Big' Tychynski, giving Mrs. Wizer no account of how he had received his injuries. Tychynski brought him into his kitchen, noticing that a black, silky rag was still tied around Louis's neck. He washed Louis's face and asked him several times who had done this to him. Louis made no reply, but asked him to call Police Chief Dennis Harold, who lived only half a mile away.

Tall, portly, twenty-one years on the force, the chief was everything a small-town policeman needed to be — affable, knowledgeable about local affairs and devious as the devil. When Louis got 'Big' Tychynski to call Chief Harold, it was no casual calling in of the local constabulary: Chief Harold was his friend and confidant. The chief was shocked at his buddy's condition. He noted the long underwear, the torn white shirt, the eyes dark and closed and the fact that Louis was holding his side in pain. 'Help me to the car, Chief. I'll show you where it happened,' said Louis. They drove to the Davis Side

175

Road nearby, looking for Louis's car, but didn't find it, so Chief Harold dropped Louis at his store, where later that morning he was seen by Dr. William MacMillan. The chief eventually found the long, sleek automobile parked in the bush. On the back seat he found two sets of keys, Louis's bank book and, most significant, a button apparently torn from a woman's coat.

Dr. MacMillan meanwhile found that Louis was badly bruised and seemed to have several broken ribs. 'Who did this to you?' he asked. 'I'll tell you later,' said Louis. The doctor ordered him into nearby Maplehurst private hospital; when he saw him there again at noon, Louis was ready to talk.

'I'm finished,' he told the doctor. 'I'm all in. I'm going to die.' The doctor pooh-poohed the idea. 'Yeah, I can't get well,' said Louis, 'And I know who did this to me. You know them, too, Doctor. It was Mrs. Johnson and her man Popovich, and they took my money.' It was not surprising that he called Liz Popovich 'Mrs. Johnson' — the name she went by before she had married George Popovich eighteen months earlier. Louis had done everything in his power to prevent the marriage.

Liz, thirty-seven, a widow with three teenaged daughters, two of them still living at home, had been Louis's mistress for several years. You wouldn't call it a romance, more a practical arrangement. She worked in his store, and sex on the side was a convenience to both parties. But marriage was never mentioned, and when George Popovich, forty-four, a hard-working, husky fellow with a regular job at the mill, came on the scene and was prepared to marry Liz and support the two daughters, she jumped ship. Louis wasn't willing to let her go. It had been so handy having her there: when trade was slack, he could give her the nod, they'd put the 'closed' sign on the door and scoot upstairs to the front bedroom. Hell, maybe he even loved her.

So, he tried every way he knew to persuade her not to marry George, including sending along his friend Chief Harold to talk to her. 'What you want to marry that Bohunk for?' he'd asked her. 'Ain't Louis been good to you?' Nothing would change her mind, she told the chief. In January 1945, with the Reverend Dr. Forster presiding, she and George were married and set up home in a two-room shanty, into which she and George and her daughters – Florence, eighteen, and Helen, fourteen – somehow managed to cram themselves.

But Louis didn't give up. And maybe it was that George, a great lug of a guy with hands like grain shovels, wasn't such a great lover. Maybe those afternoons with the 'closed' sign on the door weren't so bad after all. More likely it was that Louis had more money to spend, and she felt kind of grand rolling along in his Pierce-Arrow. But the fact was that, while George worked nights at the mill, Liz was soon taking night-time rides in the car up side roads where they could park and be private as you like in that immense backseat. And, as the months went by, Louis would say, 'Why don't you get a divorce from that guy, Liz? You need a bit of fun in your life.'

'Divorce! That's a big laugh. These lawyers cost money.'

'I'll pay. Just say the word.' And finally she agreed. Did Liz really mean to divorce George, or was it just a

177

scheme to get money out of Louis? We'll never know. But on Sunday, June 16, a day when George was due to work the night shift, she arranged to meet Louis, who had promised he'd have $200 for her to pay the lawyer. Then George, who had spent much of the day snoozing on the lawn, announced he didn't feel like going to work that night and would book off sick. While George went back to sleep, Liz slipped down to Louis's store and told him she couldn't make it for the time they'd arranged. Her only chance, she said, was to meet him later, after George was in bed.

At the Maplehurst hospital, Louis's condition worsened. A spinal tap showed blood was seeping from the brain or spinal column. Dr. MacMillan ordered him moved to the larger St. Catharine's hospital. 'I don't want to go,' Louis complained to Nurse Florence Stevenson, who owned the hospital. 'I want to die here with you and the girls. I don't want strangers looking after me.' He was also determined not to die 'without knowing Mrs. Johnson and that man she married, Popovich, are taken care of.'

The story he told the nurse and the doctor was that, at eleven o'clock on the night of the attack, George and Liz had come to his store, asking him to drive them somewhere. As they drove along the Davis Side Road in the Pierce-Arrow, he said, without warning he was hit above the eye with the heel of a woman's shoe. Blinded, he struggled to control the car as it veered from one side of the road to the other. As he brought it to a standstill, someone leaned over, switched off the motor and grabbed the keys. Then, he told them weakly, the couple had dragged him out of the car, beaten him and taken his wallet, which contained $283. Not satisfied, they pulled off his pants and searched his underwear to see if he had more money hidden there. They'd driven him farther along the road before dumping him out while the car was still in motion and giving him another beating, before leaving him tied up in a field. After several hours he'd struggled free and staggered to Mrs. Wizer's house.

His story told, Louis allowed himself to be transferred to St. Catharine's hospital where, five days after receiving the beating, he died. The pathologist, Dr. Lorne Whittaker, found Nato had suffered not only a brain hemorrhage, but seven fractured ribs and a punctured lung. He had received one hell of a drubbing, consistent, he would say in court, with someone putting the boots to him and throwing him from a moving car.

The day Louis died, the Popovichs, already facing charges of robbery with violence, were charged by Chief Harold with murder. Two days later, the chief went with Provincial Police Inspector George Mackay to the Popovich house. Under a pile of coats on a trunk in the bedroom, they found a coat with a button missing. The buttons matched the one the chief had found in Louis's car.

When the trial opened in Welland in September, the prosecution was handled by C. Hope, a crackerjack lawyer from Toronto with wide experience. The Popovichs were represented by Wendall Musgrave, a sadsack lawyer from Niagara Falls with little courtroom experience described by a contemporary reporter as 'a pauper lawyer.'

On the face of it, the crown's case was feeble. Louis had said nothing to Helen Wizer or 'Big' Tychynski, the first people he met, about who had attacked him. There were no physical marks observed on either of the defendants to indicate they had been in a fight. Nick Bugay, who lived over Louis's store, testified that he had seen Liz talking to Louis in the store the afternoon of the attack. Bugay also worked alongside Popovich in the finishing room at the mill where one-ton rolls of paper had to be moved. 'It takes a good man to budge one of those rolls,' he said, in response to a question from Hope. 'The average man can't do it.' And George Popovich? 'It don't seem to me as if he had any trouble at all with the rolls.' The only witness placing the Popovichs anywhere near the crime scene was John Kuchoruk who said he was walking home from work that night around 12:45 when he saw the couple walking in the direction of their home. George had called out, 'Hello, John.'

Even counting the evidence of the button — which could have ended up in the back of Louis's car under any number of circumstances — the case against George and Liz was pretty flimsy — except for the statements Louis Nato had made to the doctor and nurse before dying. Normally such statements would be considered hearsay and would not have been admissible as evidence. But there's a wrinkle in the law: where the victim of an attack believes himself to be near death, and does in fact die, the court can admit his dying statement. The thinking is that people don't tell lies on their deathbeds.

A good defence lawyer would have come to court with

a slew of expert witnesses prepared to argue that Louis Nato, as even Dr. MacMillan admitted, was frequently befuddled in his final days, and that he wouldn't have known what he was saying. Instead, all Musgrave offered was his own humble opinion. 'The only thing I can say, My Lord,' bleated Musgrave, 'is I believe this man was not sufficiently conscious to make all the detailed statements.'

'Does the belief of counsel matter to me!' boomed the fire-eating judge, Justice W.F. Schroeder. 'He is not even a witness.' Musgrave sat down, and Dr. MacMillan and Nurse Stevenson went into the witness box to give Louis Nato's version of what happened.

Then, the hapless Musgrave, who committed suicide a few years later, made his second big mistake in allowing his clients to go into the box to tell stories that wouldn't have fooled a baby. That night, they both claimed with straight faces, they had driven in George's car into Welland and visited with their friend, John Suich, at his taxi stand. Suich had to go off on taxi runs periodically, and when he didn't return from a run at midnight, they hung around until two before going to the Balkan Restaurant for food.

'When your friend did not return, you walked up and down until two o'clock?' said Judge Schroeder, glaring down at George. 'Yes,' he replied. The judge shook his head. 'Almost two hours, eh?'

Questioned about the coat with the missing button, Liz said at first that it belonged to her daughter, Helen, but was forced to admit it had formerly been her coat. Prosecutor Hope nailed home the point by having her try it on. 'Still a fair fit, isn't it?' he said. 'Turn around. Thank you.'

Musgrave compounded the damage by having Liz's daughters, Florence and Helen, confirm the accused couple's account. Hope destroyed them in the box with no trouble at all. Florence was forced to admit she'd lied to the police when she'd told them she hadn't heard her parents come in that night. In fact, she had seen them in the kitchen about 3:00 a.m. Helen's story was that Louis Nato had driven her to school several times when she was wearing the coat, and the button might have come off in the back seat.

'Now, witness,' said Hope, 'can you tell me what occasion there was for you to ride all alone in the back of this seven-passenger automobile with the glass between the front and rearseats, while Mr. Nato was up front driving?'

'Well,' answered Helen sheepishly, 'there was no occasion at all, I suppose.'

Now the jurors could be pretty certain the Popovichs were liars, but were they also murderers? In the absence of any other plausible explanation for their actions, and after two hours' deliberation, the answer they delivered was, yes. The words of the death sentence were hardly out of the judge's mouth when Liz's daughters ran toward the prisoners' dock. A constable quickly handcuffed George and led him out; Liz, being hustled toward the door, cried, 'I want to kiss my daughters before I go.'

A few days later, The Reverend Harvey Forster, who conducted George and Liz's wedding ceremony, responded to George's request that he visit him in jail.

'I want you to hear my confession, Reverend,' he said. Forster agreed. But the story that emerged as the two sat in the dreary visiting area in the Welland County Jail didn't resemble the story told in court at all.

He told the minister that he and Liz had come home from Welland around midnight. She had disappeared as soon as they got in, and a few minutes later he had seen a car glide by, which he was sure was Louis Nato's Pierce-Arrow. George must have been harbouring suspicions about his wife, because he immediately jumped into his 1928 Buick and took off in pursuit. Switching off his headlights, George had come upon the Pierce-Arrow parked beside the Davis Side Road, had gotten out and had discovered his wife making love with Nato. At that point his Slavic temper took over: he thumped Louis in the face. Louis was no pushover: he lashed out with his foot and kicked George in the groin. George still had the hernia from that kick; however, it hadn't prevented his yanking Louis out of the car. As Liz ran home, these two powerful men flailed and kicked at each other, grunting and staggering in the dark. George, spurred by his anger and outrage, was the winner.

Louis, he told the minister, offered him money not to beat him any more, but he'd spurned it. When Louis came crying and wailing after him as he walked away, claimed George, he had tied him with a rope and gagged him. At that point, he admitted, he had taken Louis's money, which still lay on the ground. Cowering in a shed behind their home, Liz must have been expecting that she, too, would be beaten. Instead, George, when he found her, ordered her into the car, and they drove into Welland with

183

the clear intention of cooking up an alibi. When Forster visited Liz in the women's section of the prison, she told him exactly the same story, even though she hadn't seen her husband since the day they were sentenced and had had no opportunity to compare stories.

Forster, though he wasn't a lawyer, immediately saw the importance of the new evidence. If the court had heard that George attacked Louis because he'd found his wife in the other man's arms, then most likely he would have been found guilty only of manslaughter — which did not carry the death penalty. And Liz, if she took no part in the attack, should not be in jail at all.

The new evidence was submitted at their appeal. To no effect. 'It would be a travesty of justice,' declared Chief Justice J.R. Robertson, 'to allow people to come forward, state their whole defence was a prepared lie, and say, 'We perjured ourselves by swearing it.' The only evidence you are seeking to produce,' he told the Popovichs' lawyers, 'does not contradict what the crown proved — that is that they killed this man.' Killing is killing, the chief justice was saying. Don't bother me with details.

In desperation, Forster went to see Chief Harold. Only then he learned that Louis Nato, on the morning that Harold had driven him back to the scene of the attack, had told him that Popovich had beaten him after finding him with his wife. Then why on earth hadn't the chief said that when he had testified at the trial! Ah, said the chief wisely, he couldn't do that. That would only be hearsay, wouldn't it? The fact was that Chief Harold, and presumably the prosecutor, had known that Louis Nato had lied on his death bed.

184

With all legal recourse at an end, Forster now began a desperate campaign for a reprieve, gathering signatures and firing off petitions to Justice Minister St. Laurent. Nato's dying statements to the nurse and doctor just didn't make sense, he argued in his submissions. Why would the Popovichs ask Louis to take them for a drive in his car at 11:00 p.m. that fatal night when they had a car of their own? How could Louis know in the dark that he had been struck by the heel of a woman's shoe? And who, anyway, would try to stun someone with such a flimsy weapon? Why would a couple rob a man who knew them well? And why, most important of all, would they leave him alive when they knew he would blow the whistle on them as soon as he got back to town? (It would also be fair to ask why George Popovich felt it was necessary to have an alibi, since Louis was still alive and was not likely to report that attack to the police.)

Forster even went to Ottawa, button-holed members of parliament, and saw a senior Justice department official after failing to get an appointment with St. Laurent. 'Father was terribly upset by the whole thing,' Forster's son, George, now living in Toronto, told me. 'He believed the system would not allow this to happen.' But, reading through the Popovich file in the National Archives in Ottawa, I could see that, apart from Forster, no one was concerned that a tragic injustice might be done. Judge Schroeder, in his private report to the justice minister, said, 'There was undoubtedly a murder committed by these accused, and it was a calculated, cold-blooded murder with robbery as its chief, if not only, motive.'

Chief Harold reported smugly to the commissioner of the Royal Canadian Mounted Police that, on searching the Popovich home further, he had discovered more evidence against the couple – Louis Nato's watch and rope similar to that used to tie him, both concealed in the house. 'This whole case was premeditated and arranged by Mrs. Popovich,' he wrote, perhaps feeling that he had now avenged his friend's death.

But, in the end, Harvey Forster's pleadings may have come closer to swaying the government than he realized. Scanning the file, I came across a strange anomaly. On the letterhead of the Minister of Justice is a note addressed to 'His Excellency the Governor General in Council' – in effect the cabinet – in which the minister recommends the death penalty should be commuted to life imprisonment for both George and Liz. Searching further, I came upon a document that is identical – except for the final recommendation: that the law be allowed to take its course. There is no explanation for the two conflicting reports, and archivists could recall no similar situation in a capital case. Whatever the arguments that went on in cabinet, whatever last-minute doubts the government may have entertained, on November 28, the governor general, Viscount Alexander of Tunis, signed the approval for the death sentence to be carried out. Forster was informed by telegram on December 4, the day before the execution date.

Even as he prepared to go to the jail to be with the Popovichs at the end, Forster was still trying to reach St. Laurent in New York. Finally he was put through. The

186

minister said he could do nothing. 'He was quite curt and brusque with my father,' Forster's son recalled.

The cell blocks in Welland County Jail where George and Elizabeth Popovich spent their last weeks are no longer in use. The county registrar, Dave Thomas, led me through dark, smelly, half-flooded passageways to show me a cell with a completely boarded-up doorway and no electric light inside where Liz was sometimes confined when she became distraught. I retraced the few steps they would have taken leading them into the prison yard where the scaffold had been erected. There is no record of whether, together at last, they held hands as they crossed the yard, with Forster leading the way, reading the Lord's Prayer. But, as she reached the top of the steps, Liz turned to the jury there to witness the execution and cried, 'God bless you all.' She was the only woman ever executed in the Welland County Jail.

George Forster says his father, who had worked with the poor in the slums of New York as a young man, regarded the execution as 'one of the most distressing things that ever happened in his life. The thing that shocked him was that the system didn't work.'

It's not hard to see why. The Popovichs were people of little account, living in a part of the country the rest of Canada preferred to ignore. They had a foreign name and, with the exception of Harvey Forster, had no prominent people to stand up for them, no eminent lawyers vying for the defence brief. Their execution was the culmination of a series of blunders. It was George's misplaced manly pride that probably prevented him from coming clean from the start and admitting his wife had deceived him. Equally, it was Louis Nato's pride — and an urge for revenge — that prevented him from admitting he had been beaten in a fight over another man's wife. And Elizabeth? She was unfaithful and maybe even a scheming trickster out to cheat Louis Nato. But adultery isn't a hanging offence — is it?

A VIXEN
CORNERED

Elizabeth Popovich paid the ultimate price for flouting sexual conventions. But, as Florence Bravo discovered, society has other ways of pushing those who break the moral rules. The poisoning of her husband, Charles, provided the nineteenth century with perhaps its greatest unsolved murder mystery. But it's fair to ask whether the spotlight of suspicion would have been shone so relentlessly on Florence if she had not been a sexual rebel, ahead of her times. You can still visit the scene of the crime, a battlemented Victorian mansion called The Priory on Bedford Hill Road, in Balham, an inner suburb of London. A few years ago it had lapsed into a ruin, but now it's been converted into expensive flats, and the bedroom where Bravo died is someone's living room.

The house's gothic windows still look out across the lush park and to the stand of oaks where Charles went riding that day, and at the top of the stairs there's still a portrait of Florence in slightly precious pose, the tips of her fingers touching her cheek, the mouth petulant, the wide eyes gazing into the hazy distance.

'A little rich girl who went off the tracks,' was how Kate Clarke, who, with Bernard Taylor, has published a study of the case, *Murder at The Priory*, described her to me. But does that do her justice? It seems to me it took a lot of gumption for a young woman of those times to defy her parents and society in following her heart.

Her spirit of independence may have stemmed from the fact she was a colonial girl, born in New South Wales on September 5, 1845, the daughter of Anne and Robert Campbell. Robert had inherited a fortune from his father, who had been active in sheep farming and gold mining, and in 1859 the couple moved to England, where Campbell set up his family in splendid Buscot Park, an eighteenth-century mansion in Berkshire.

Florence's first matrimonial venture was as conventional as her parents could have hoped: while on a visit to Montreal with her parents, she met a young Grenadier Guards officer, Captain Alexander Ricardo, and, in 1864 − she nineteen, he twenty-one, they were married at the village church in Buscot by the Bishop of Oxford. Both families made handsome marriage settlements, and the young couple went off to honeymoon on the Rhine, their lives, most people would have said, already mapped out for them.

That Florence did not conform to the needlework-and-childcare pattern adopted by millions of other women of her era is probably traceable to one factor alone: young Ricardo was a boozer. And after putting up with his drinking binges for several years, Florence sought temporary relief in the healing waters at Malvern, where she renewed her acquaintance with a fashionable physician, Dr. James Manby Gully, whom she and her sister had met while still at school, and who had treated such eminences as Florence Nightingale, Alfred Tennyson and Charles Dickens.

At sixty-two, Dr. Gully was more than twice Florence's age, but as his hydropathic treatments and, more important, his sympathetic personality brought relief to her strained nerves, she found herself more and more drawn to the doctor. He gave her the support and comfort so plainly missing from her marriage, while Dr. Gully, whose wife had, for years, been in an asylum, found in her the female companionship long absent from his life.

Florence, recognizing the impossibility of this attraction, did attempt a reconciliation with her husband, but following a violent episode and defying her father, she officially separated from Ricardo and consulted a lawyer recommended by Dr. Gully.

Soon afterwards, Ricardo died, leaving Florence at age twenty-six with her youth and looks intact and with a substantial inheritance. Fortunately, considering the suspicion that later surrounded Florence following the death of her second husband, Ricardo died in Germany while she was in England.

With Ricardo's death, the obstacle preventing the relationship with Dr. Gully was removed. Cold-shouldered by her parents, Florence rented a villa in Streatham, on the outskirts of London, while Dr. Gully, now retired, rented a house close by. Soon the couple were seen socially together, and scandalized their families and friends by spending six weeks in Italy unchaperoned. At this point, the third member of the trio that would soon be the focus of world-wide attention – and suspicion – arrived on the scene. Jane Cox, a former children's governess, born in the East Indies, and with three children of her own to support, answered an advertisement placed by Florence for a paid companion. For her generous salary, Mrs. Cox obligingly turned a blind eye too Florence's affair with Dr. Gully, even to the extent, in 1873, of keeping quiet when she had to nurse Florence following an abortion performed by Dr. Gully.

Soon after her recovery, Florence moved to The Priory in Balham, in South London, and Dr. Gully rented a yellow three-storey house just ten minutes' walk away. But even a woman of Florence's independent set could not indefinitely endure the social ostracism she suffered. She had grown up in the world of balls and afternoon teas, of gossip and constant invitations. What was the sense of being rich and beautiful if you were restricted to the company of one elderly, if charming admirer and a paid companion?

By the summer of 1875 she had resolved to break her ties with Dr. Gully, but lacked the courage to tell him. Then, during a stay at Brighton, an excuse presented itself in the form of Charles Bravo, a lawyer and family acquaintance whom she ran into on the promenade. In her letters to Charles, who, at thirty, was the same age as she, Florence seems quite determined that their relationship should ripen into engagement and marriage, and young Bravo needed little encouragement.

Several authors have suggested Bravo, who liked a flutter on the stock market, had his eye strictly on Florence's fortune. But it must be remembered Florence was a highly attractive woman, and it would be truer to say that he was drawn to her, even captivated by her, and at the same time found her money no deterrent.

There was still Dr. Gully to be disposed of. When he visited her in Brighton, she could not bring herself to tell him, and imparted the news to him in a letter which he received on his return to Balham. The doctor was shocked, and insisted on seeing her again. The interview was painful on both sides, and Dr. Gully's chagrin was not lessened when, riding through Brighton they passed Charles Bravo who raised his hat to Florence. She admitted he was the man she was seeing. Telling Charles about the doctor, however, proved an easier task after the young lawyer admitted to his sweetheart that he had been having an affair with a woman in Maidenhead for several years. He could not conceive of a doddering doctor in his sixties as a serious rival for Florence's affections, and in October 1875, to the great relief of Florence's parents, the couple became engaged.

There was one last-minute hitch. Florence, a woman ahead of her time, insisted, to Charles's disgust, that a marriage contract be drawn up allowing her, contrary to the custom of the time, to retain title to her fortune. Money, it turned out, would be a constant bone of contention after the couple was married at Kensington in December 1875.

Charles was the take-charge sort. Not only was he soon impatient with Florence's extravagance — regarding Mrs. Cox's salary, for example — but he also consulted a doctor about what he regarded as her excessive drinking.

Although it was not a marriage made in heaven, there

seems to have been genuine love and affection on both sides. When Florence had a miscarriage ten weeks after they were married and took a short holiday at St.-Leonards-on-sea to recuperate, Charles wrote, 'I miss you, my darling wife, dreadfully . . . We have had bitter troubles, but I trust that in times to come the sweet peace of our lives will not be disturbed by memories like these.'

On April 6, Florence suffered another miscarriage. Word reached Dr. Gully, still living a short walk away, that she was experiencing sleeplessness and back pain, and he sent along a bottle of cherry laurel water, a soothing agent.

The morning of April 18, Florence was feeling better and drove into town with Charles in their landau. While he had a Turkish bath and met her uncle for lunch, Florence went shopping, buying a hair wash (an early form of shampoo) and tobacco for Charles before returning home for lunch.

Arriving home by train soon after 4:30 p.m., Charles announced he was going riding. He expressed pleasure when he found in his dressing room the small purchases Florence had made for him earlier in the day. But the ride did not go well: Charles returned home shaken and unwell after his horse had bolted, and Florence insisted he have a warm bath before dinner.

The evening meal, as was often the case, was a tense occasion. Charles, already feeling out of sorts, was incensed at a 'shirty' letter he had just received from his father, criticizing him for speculating on the stock market, and was also upset about a cheque to a tradesman that Mrs. Cox claimed to have mailed, but that had gone astray. Throughout dinner — whiting, roast lamb, eggs and anchovies — he watched disapprovingly as Florence and Mrs. Cox between them consumed two bottles of sherry. When, after Florence had gone to her room, he saw the maid carrying a second tumbler of Marsala wine and water up to her, he could no longer contain his impatience. In her dressing room, he upbraided her for her drinking, using French so the maid would not understand.

Charles, in deference to Florence's ill-health, and perhaps to give her a break after two miscarriages, was sleeping in the bedroom next to hers. When he left her, she was already getting woozily into bed, while Mrs Cox, in attendance, was still dressed. But Charles's door was closed only for a few minutes before it was again thrown open, and Charles, now in his nightshirt, stood in the hallway crying, 'Florence! Florence! Hot water! Hot water!'

Mrs. Cox, running out of Florence's room, found him by now standing at his bedroom window, retching and vomiting onto the roof of the bay window below. Again he cried for water, and Mrs. Cox sent the maid scurrying for it. When she returned, Charles was sitting unconscious on the floor while Mrs. Cox was rubbing his chest. This time she sent the maid for mustard and, when she brought it, grabbed the container, mixed some with water in a tumbler and tried to force Charles to drink. When this failed, she sent the maid for strong coffee, of which he was able to swallow a little before vomiting again into a bowl. Mrs. Cox ordered the maid to wash the bowl, went downstairs and dispatched the

195

groom for Mr. Harrison, the family physician, in Streatham.

Through all this commotion, Florence slept on, we can only assume, in a drunken stupor. When she was finally wakened and saw Charles's condition, she burst into tears. But she had enough presence of mind to send for a doctor who lived close by.

By 2:30 a.m., there were four doctors at Charles Bravo's bedside, all of them equally puzzled by his symptoms. Mrs. Cox, with apparent reluctance, told them that, in those first minutes after she had found him, Charles had told her, 'I've taken poison. Don't tell Florence.'

But Charles, as he lingered in agony, would say only that he had rubbed laudanum, an opium preparation used commonly in those days, into his gums to ease soreness. The doctors did not believe for a moment that this had caused his illness..

After three days of suffering, Charles summoned his family and servants together, said prayers and bade them farewell. He died early the following morning, with Florence and Mrs. Cox at his side. Analysis of the vomit collected from the roof slates by one of the doctors early on the scene would show that Charles Bravo had taken antimony, an irritant poison.

And there we have it: was it suicide or murder? And, if murder, who was responsible – Florence? Dr. Gully? Mrs. Cox? All three?

Strings were pulled by the shocked family, and at a quick and discreet inquest in the dining room at The Priory, a jury of local tradesmen returned an open verdict.

But nothing could prevent such a juicy affair coming to public attention, and James Bravo, Charles's father, for one, was not satisfied that all the facts were known.

Newspapers carried reports of what was now known as 'The Balham Mystery'; anonymous letters full of accusations arrived at The Priory; and finally, on July 11, nearly three months after Charles's death, a new inquest attended by vast publicity and a legion of lawyers representing the interests of nearly everyone involved opened in the billiard room of the nearby Bedford Hotel. To the delight of the newspaper-reading public, everyone with the least connection to the case was questioned exhaustively, and every last piece of what William Roughhead, the dean of true-crime writers, would call 'the prize puzzle of British criminal jurisprudence' was brought into the open for examination.

Dr. Gully, it was learned, had made a large purchase of an antimony preparation for his horses four years previously, and, further, Charles had strongly suspected Dr. Gully of sending an anonymous letter exposing Florence's earlier affair with the doctor and accusing Charles of marrying her for her money.

Jane Cox, it transpired, had, shortly before Charles died, received a letter from an aunt in Jamaica asking her to come there immediately so that she could discuss leaving her property to one of Mrs. Cox's three sons, a development the relevance of which we shall see shortly. And there was ample evidence that, considering they had been married only a few months, there was a good deal of ill will between the husband and wife as Charles tried to impose limits on Florence's drinking and spending. In

197

the end, the jurors decided Charles had been murdered. By whom they were not prepared to say, and no one was ever charged.

In her day, Florence was the popular scapegoat. She had defied society's mores by having an affair with Dr. Gully; she was rich, self-indulgent — she even dyed her hair red — and when she died two years later of alcoholism, it was easy for the public to believe she drank herself to death out of a sense of remorse.

Writers since have also made her their favourite suspect. John Williams, in his book *Suddenly at The Priory*, argues that Florence, 'ruthless, self-centred, supremely unsentimental,' realized that in marrying Charles Bravo she had made a terrible mistake that would cost her her freedom, a mistake that could be remedied only with his death.

Historian Elizabeth Jenkins has put forward the hypothesis that, after suffering two miscarriages, Florence dreaded further sexual contact with Charles and killed him by mistake when, adding tartar of emetic to his water to make him sick and unable to perform, she accidentally overdosed him.

Other writers, including Agatha Christie — herself an expert in poisons — have pointed the finger at Dr. Gully. He had antimony available in his stables and, with the connivance of Mrs. Cox or one of the servants, would not have found it difficult to arrange for it to be put into Charles's water bottle in his bedroom. Even if Dr. Gully was no longer seeing Florence, there is evidence he was in contact with Mrs. Cox, who would have looked back fondly on the time of the Gully regime at The Priory, comparing it favourably with that marred by Charles Bravo's intrusive and threatening presence.

Kate Clarke doesn't believe Dr. Gully played any part in the murder. He had long given up any hope of rekindling the affair with Florence, she said, and revenge on Charles Bravo, the man who had supplanted him, hardly seems a likely motive for a man noted for his kindly nature.

And, in spite of what the public thought at the time, Clarke sees Florence as the unlikeliest suspect. 'She made him a pair of slippers. She could have ordered them from Harrods, but she made them,' she said. 'People don't generally make slippers for people they are planning to murder.' She had disagreements with her husband, 'but don't all couples? She was a silly woman, but I think they got on quite well.'

We had talked past the supper hour in Clarke's small cottage in Hay-on-Wye. Clarke got up and closed the half-door through which the Black Mountains beyond had faded from vivid green to shadow. 'I am absolutely sure,' she said, turning, 'that Mrs. Cox did it. Charles Bravo resented the extravagance of keeping Mrs. Cox on now that he and Florence were married, and he would have seen her as a reminder of his wife's earlier affair with Dr. Gully. He must also have believed it would be easier to wean Florence from the bottle if she did not have Mrs. Cox as a drinking companion.

'Mrs. Cox feared her days in Florence's employ were numbered,' said Clarke, 'and then the letter from her aunt, urging her to come to Jamaica, had put her in a

199

terrible quandary. If she went, and was away for several months, she could be sure there would be no job waiting for her when she returned. At the same time, if she didn't go, her son might lose out on the aunt's inheritance. In this complicated human chess game, only the removal of one of the pieces – Charles Bravo – would secure her position. Cox,' said Clarke, 'had the opportunity to put antimony into Charles Bravo's water bottle after dinner. She would have bargained on Florence dropping off and then would have been waiting, ears alert, for the first sound of distress from Charles's room. It must have come even sooner than she expected, and she went into lightning action.

'By sending the maid to fetch water and mustard, she gave herself time to wash out the water bottle and to clean up any incriminating evidence. By dispatching the groom for the doctor, who lived several miles away, she intended to allow more time for the poison to work.

'But,' said Clarke, 'there were two things she hadn't allowed for. Charles did not, as might have been expected, die immediately from heart failure, but lingered on for three days. And by vomiting on the roof, where she was unable to remove the evidence, he provided the proof that he was poisoned.'

Mrs. Cox, who, in fact, sailed for Jamaica soon after the inquest, had three boys to support at boarding school. 'She was a cornered vixen with cubs,' said Clarke, 'and she fought back.'

MURDER
FOR LOVE

She was not so young. Attractive, yes, in that French way, with the hair piled on top of her head and the eyes large and expressive. The lips, too, had that slightly pouty, voluptuous look. You couldn't say it was lines or wrinkles that suggested her age so much as a certain sadness that crept over her features when she was not being consciously vivacious.

' 'Ere, 'ere, what's the little nipper crying for?' said the omnibus conductor, appearing at her shoulder. 'What's the matter, then, my little ducky?'

'I don't want to go,' sobbed Manfred. 'I don't want to go.'

'What's got into 'im then? Breakin' 'is little 'eart, 'e is.'

'He is going to see his father. In France, you know,' said Louise. 'Come on, darling, please don't cry.'

'Goin' to France, is it then? Ooh, ain't you the lucky one,' beamed the conductor. 'Wish I was goin' too, ooh-la-la!' Manfred, who was three-and-a-half, turned toward the window and began to kick the back of the seat in front.

'Don't, darling, please,' said Louise. 'I want one-and-a-half to London Bridge station, please,' she told the conductor.

She stared out of the window at the Friday-afternoon crowds milling around the costermongers' barrows, but she could see only his face. He loved her, she was sure of that. He had said it so many times. *Eudore!* She said his name in her mind for the thousandth time. And tomorrow morning she would see him again. That's what she must think about, not the . . . other thing. He was so young, only nineteen, and so romantic. That first day, when she had been sitting in the garden at Stoke Newington she was not even aware of his existence. Then she had heard his voice: 'Excuse me, Mademoiselle . . . Hello!' She could see only the top of his head through the trellis at the top of the fence. 'Mademoiselle, would you accept this, please?' He was pushing a folded sheet of paper through the golden yellow roses.

'Oh, be careful. You will scratch your hand,' she called. 'Is it a note for my sister?'

'No, it is for you. Perhaps you would be kind enough to read it when you have a moment.' His English was impeccable but the accent was unmistakably French. Louise, whose father was French, had grown up in France, but she had lived in England so long she now barely had an accent. Thanking the young man, she had taken the note to her room before unfolding it. It was a poem he had written.

'London Bridge!' the conductor shouted. Louise grabbed her Gladstone bag, surprised for an instant by the weight of it. 'Come along, darling,' she said, taking

Manfred's hand. He was moaning and sighing deep sobbing breaths. Perhaps the trains would distract him.

'Look,' she said as they crossed the smoky concourse a few minutes later. 'Look at the choo-choos.' A bright green Southern Railway locomotive came sighing into the station, puffing sweet-smelling coal smoke, and came to a standstill with a snort of steam.

'I don't want to go,' whimpered Manfred.

'Now, my little love,' said the large, motherly-looking attendant in the first-class ladies' waiting room. 'We can't 'ave you carrying on like that. Would you like a sweetie?' From the pocket of her apron she produced a packet of wine gums and squeezed one out for Manfred. Temporarily distracted, he stopped crying.

'He's missing his nurse,' Louise told her. 'Usually he's such a good boy.'

'Perhaps 'e's 'ungry,' the woman suggested.

'Yes, perhaps so. Is there a refreshment bar nearby? I would like to get him a cake.' Something odd about the woman, thought Mrs. Rees, the attendant, as Louise led Manfred away in the direction of the refreshment bar. She seemed so anxious, then hurried away as if she didn't want to talk. Ah well, she thought, returning to her knitting, it takes all sorts.

'Dalston Junction? That train on the left,' said the man on the gate, looking at her ticket.

'I know,' said Louise. She had travelled this way so often on her way to tutor the Haas girls. It used to be a dreary journey past the sooty warehouses of the East End, but since Eudore began stealing time away from his job with the bank almost every day to accompany her to Dalston Junction, her life had begun to revolve around these magic half-hour trips.

'It is our secret affair,' he would say, enjoining her not to tell her sister and brother-in-law, with whom she boarded in Stoke Newington. She was so proud to take his arm at London Bridge, him so smart, carrying his silk hat and suede gloves like any city toff. True, he was only earning a clerk's salary of £3 a month, but he was over from Paris to train in the financial business, and undoubtedly a fine career lay ahead of him. They had not actually discussed marriage – on Eudore's salary that would be ludicrous. But, at night, in her room, with only the wall between the houses separating them, Louise Masset would imagine herself, not meeting surreptitiously on the train or stealing weekends together in the cheapest Brighton hotels, but on his arm at important social functions in Paris and proud to be introduced as 'Madame Lucas.' And only one thing, she was convinced, stood between her and that vision of what might be; only one obstacle lay in the path of their happiness.

Of course, Eudore had been understanding about Manfred. He was not bothered at all when she explained – as was only fair – that he was the result of a failed romance and that Manfred's father, now back in France, paid for his upkeep at the home of Miss Helen Gentle, a children's nurse. 'I do not need to know any more. It is forgotten,' Eudore assured her. But she knew that some day Manfred must stand in the way of her marriage. How could Eudore bring her home to meet his parents when she had a child out of wedlock?

The train was slowing down. The large sign sliding past

the window said 'Dalston Junction.' As she did up the buttons on Manfred's little navy-blue sailor coat, her hands were trembling.

At 6:20 p.m. that day, Joe Standing, a porter at Dalston Junction, had just come back on duty after eating his supper of tomato and cucumber sandwiches when two respectable-looking women approached him. 'You'd better check. There's a woman been taken ill in the ladies' room on platform three,' the older woman told him. Wondering mildly why they hadn't helped the woman themselves, Standing ran down the steps to the platform.

'Hello!' he called, standing outside the door. 'Can I help? Are you all right?' No sound came from within. He called a few more times, knocked, then opened the door. Inside was what appeared to be a bundle wrapped in a black shawl. He opened it gingerly, then gasped. It was the naked body of a child, the head bloodied. On the floor beside it lay a brick made from clinker, broken in two. The porter raced back up the stairs to give the alarm. There was no sign of the two women.

The newspapers headlined it 'Terrible Discovery at Dalston Junction.' Called to the scene, Dr. J.P. Fennell had found the body still warm, they reported, and estimated the boy had been killed less than an hour before. Death, he would later say, had been caused by someone stunning the child with the brick and then holding a hand or some other object over his mouth and nose until he suffocated.

The identity of the child was a mystery, as was the intent of the murderer. No one had noticed anyone accompanying a child through the barrier at Dalston

205

Junction, although, it was pointed out, they could have gotten off a train stopping at the station and the murderer could have reboarded it or got on another train immediately afterwards. Then, after reading a description of the child's clothing, Miss Helen Gentle, a children's nurse from Tottenham, in South London, contacted the police. After being shown the body, she covered her face. Yes, she said, the child was Manfred Louis Masset, and he had been in her care until the previous Friday. His mother had taken him away, saying he was going to France, where his father would have him cared for by a cousin. Miss Gentle had been just as upset as Manfred at the parting.

Louise Masset was not at home when police called at her sister's. After reading in the newspaper that the child had been identified, she had fled to the home of another married sister, telling her, 'I'm hunted for murder, but I didn't do it.' There she was arrested and charged with murder.

By the time she appeared in the dock at the Old Bailey in December 1899 — two months after the murder — Louise Masset had recovered her composure. Speaking with a certain tremulousness and with rapid movement of the hands, she told the jury that, early in October, she had been sitting in the park while Manfred played with a little girl. She got into conversation with the two women accompanying the girl and, noticing that she wore no wedding band, one of them asked her, 'Are you married?' She admitted she wasn't, and told them Manfred was being cared for by a nurse. Was she satisfied with the care? asked the older woman, who had said she had been recently widowed. 'Oh yes,' replied Louise, 'except for his education.' You could tell by the way Manfred said 'ain't' and 'them things' that he was picking up bad speech habits, she said.

Perhaps, then, said the widow, she would like to entrust the little boy to her care. She was planning to look after two children, and the younger woman, her sister-in-law, would educate them. The cost would be only £18 a year – less than Miss Gentle was charging. Louise said she met the women again the following week and, hearing they were taking a house in King's Road, Chelsea, she completed arrangements with them. She made the excuse to Miss Gentle that Manfred was going to France so that her feelings would not be hurt.

By prearrangement, she told the court, she met the two women on the platform at London Bridge. She had planned to go with them to the King's Road house, but they were late and she had to catch a train to Brighton, so she handed over Manfred and £12 advance payment. When she asked for a receipt for the money, one of the women, whose name, she said, was Browning, said she would go to the refreshment counter to see if she could borrow a pen and ink, and paper. 'Wouldn't Manfred like a cake?' the other woman asked, and the two had left with the little boy. When they did not return, she looked in the refreshment room and, not seeing them, caught the four o'clock train to Brighton.

In a way, Louise Masset's story was plausible. This was an era when what were then termed 'baby farms' were a notorious feature of the underworld. Women in her position would sometimes answer newspaper advertisements offering baby care. A large payment would be demanded up front, and the babies would disappear – murdered. In one horrible case, babies' corpses started turning up in the River Thames. Often the mother would be just as glad to have the child taken off her hands, no questions asked. And who, anyway, were those two women who gave the alarm at Dalston Junction?

But the evidence was very much against Louise. Mrs. Rees, the attendant at London Bridge, swore she had seen Louise a second time that day, washing her hands at the station at about seven in the evening. She was alone at the time. She even picked Louise out in a lineup. The brick found beside Manfred's body matched those in a grotto in the garden at Stoke Newington. A weigh-scale, Manfred's favourite toy, which he carried with him from Miss Gentle's and which you would have thought would have gone with him to his new home, was found in Louise's bedroom, and, most damning of all, his blue serge frock and his little navy blue coat were found in a parcel in the ladies' waiting room in Brighton Station. The braid and buttons had been cut off, apparently to make identification more difficult.

Despite the evidence, Louise Masset might have gotten off. With a murder conviction carrying an automatic death penalty, juries were loath to convict a woman, especially if she was young, attractive and from the middle classes. (Overwhelmingly, women who went to the gallows in the last century were from the lower classes.) Jurors might have found it in their hearts to forgive a ruined woman with an illegitimate child to care for. But one sin society could not forgive was sexual waywardness.

208

The fact was that, when Mrs. Rees last saw her, Louise was on her way to Brighton, where Eudore Lucas was to join her the next morning for a weekend of frolic. In the witness box, Eudore, immaculate in dark coat and carrying hat and gloves, related how, a few days after their first contact, he had gone to Brighton for the Whitsun holiday with Louise and another couple. After that he and Louise began to 'walk out.'

Yes, he confirmed, she had told him about Manfred. 'I thought it very fair of her to tell me.' She had even told him her age although she had shaved a couple of years from the age revealed on her birth certificate. 'The question of marriage,' he said, 'had never been discussed between us.' Because of his small salary, 'I was in no position to marry.'

The weekend of the murder, he testified, they had reserved adjoining rooms at Finlay's Hotel in Brighton in the names of Mr. and Miss Brooke. He had noticed nothing unusual in her behaviour.

In the witness box, under the tutelage of her counsel, Lord Coleridge, Louise spoke fondly of Manfred, remembering the 'precious moments' with him in the park on her days off every Wednesday. 'I am quite prepared to give you his father's name,' she said, holding herself erect.

'Never mind his name,' said her lawyer hurriedly.

She told of the poem handed over the fence. Marriage? She laughed at the suggestion. 'It would have been absurd. Why, he's only earning two or three pounds a month! He's only nineteen and he has not served his time in the French army, as he is required to do.' Was there any truth

209

in the suggestion she had carried a brick in her Gladstone bag? 'I could not have carried the bag all that way if there was a brick in it,' she replied.

Observed the crown attorney, Sir Charles Matthews: 'One may pause a moment to admire or, to be more correct, to deplore the prisoner's great ingenuity. To the nerve of iron which was required to commit the crime must be added the tongue of a serpent.'

As the judge summed up, Louise Masset rocked back and forth on her chair in apparent anguish, and when the guilty verdict was announced, she swooned. After she was revived, reported *The Times*, 'His Lordship sentenced her to death in the usual form.'

In those days justice moved swiftly. Manfred died in October, Louise was tried in December, and her execution was set for January 9 at Newgate. A petition to Queen Victoria to spare her life was got up by French governesses working in London; in it, they said, referring to the Boer War, which was taking place at that time, 'too much blood is flowing at this hour. Act so that a woman shall not contribute to this accursed torrent.' But the queen, mindful no doubt of the outrage Louise's carryings on with Eudore had caused, held her peace, and as London fizzed and sparkled, welcoming in the new century, Louise prepared to make her departure.

An inspector of prisons, writing in her memoirs, said that Louise had confessed in her death cell to killing Manfred because she could not stand the shame of his illegitimacy. I don't believe that quite covers the facts. Manfred was already more than three years old. If his lack of an acknowledged father was such a blot, why did she not kill him earlier? Manfred was killed, I believe, because of a tragic misunderstanding. In love and, at thirty-six, losing her looks, Louise saw marriage with the young Frenchman as her last chance, and Manfred as the one obstacle preventing that. From his behaviour, though, it seems obvious that Eudore regarded his affair with Louise merely as a rather exciting fling with an older woman to spice his first assignment abroad.

A full-page newspaper illustration of the time satisfied public sentiment against Louise Masset by showing her being prepared for execution, with the hangman placing the rope around her slender neck while an assistant adjusted the strap that held her billowing skirt around her knees.

A few days after the execution, Miss Gentle was in court again, as Louise's sister was seeking to recover Manfred's toys from her. Her business, Miss Gentle complained to the magistrate, had been quite ruined because it had been said in court that she was uneducated and little Manfred had used 'ain't' and 'them things.'

'Who made these charges against her?' asked the magistrate.

'Miss Masset said it in the witness box,' was the reply.

'I am sure if the jury did not believe her, no one else would,' remarked the magistrate dryly.

London Bridge station, where Louise took Manfred on his last journey, has gone trendy now. Little boutiques tempt commuters, and the dingy old refreshment bar has been replaced by a fancy coffee shop. To get an idea of the station's original Victorian gloom, you must venture

211

down a set of stairs directing travellers to the 'London Dungeon.' Here, under great, black brick arches permeated by an acrid damp cellar smell, is Britain's scariest museum, outdoing, by far, Madame Tussaud's chamber of horrors. Beneath the station, lit by sputtering candles, is portrayed a history of torture, complete with gushing blood, ingenious machines and lifelike screams. Nothing to my ears, though, sounds as pathetic as a small child's voice saying, 'I don't want to go.'

CHOCOLATE
SURPRISE

Love, as we have seen in the case of Louise Masset, can be the great delusion, leading even to murder. And one crisp, clear January morning I went to Brighton to learn how unrequited love, that most painful disease of the heart, had once put a whole town in terror. Brighton, of course, where the Prince Regent nearly two centuries ago set the pace for illicit romance with Mrs. Fitzherbert, and where ever since couples have gone seeking satisfaction away from prying eyes, seems an unlikely place to go looking for unconsummated romance. But, walking along the sea front, where only the cars introduce a discordant twentieth-century note, it was not hard to picture the time when Mrs. Ann Edmunds promenaded here daily (weather permitting) with her daughter, Christiana, and to imagine the moment when Christiana caught the eye of fortyish Dr. Charles Beard and mistook his glance for romantic interest.

Turning my back on the sea, I made my way through the fashionable Lanes, the narrow streets where, you fancy, a Regency dandy might emerge at any moment from one of the little shops, and past the Brighton Pavilion, the Prince Regent's onion-domed attempt at turning Brighton into Baghdad-by-the-sea. My destination was Grand Parade, a handsome row of villas across the street that has seen better days.

The house I was looking for is now part of Brighton Polytechnic, a modern abomination of a building, sitting like a wart on the town's Regency face. The house where Dr. Beard lived and practised medicine in the 1870s is now one of several Grand Parade villas that serve as offices for the school. The hallway where patients would have hung their coats now has a shabby, institutional look. But the drawing room is still there — a faculty office now — and, standing behind the bow window with your eyes narrowed a little, it's not hard to imagine Emily Beard entertaining her guests to afternoon tea.

'Another piece of Dundee cake, Miss Edmunds?'

'No, thank you, dear Mrs. Beard. It was delicious,' Christiana replies, in that musical voice of hers. 'But do have one of my chocolate creams. They're French, you know.'

Do not, dear Mrs. Beard, accept her chocolates. Not on any account. Oh, no! Don't eat it, Mrs. Beard, please. Oh dear. Oh dear.

Chocolates occupy a special place in the British psyche. They are Mother, Fireside and Home, all in one succulent mouthful. Someone who would tamper with chocolates, inject poison into chocolate creams, would have to be a very bad person indeed. Or, as Christiana Edmunds was, a person very badly in love. That love would drive her

214

to try to poison half the town in a crime that has its modern parallel in the Tylenol murder of seven people in Chicago in 1982.

Christiana lived with her widowed mother in Gloucester Place in a part of Brighton called Kemp Town. There, in the eighteenth century, Mr. Kemp, had built Georgian terraces to rival, and he hoped, exceed in grandeur, those of Bath. Mrs. Edmunds, whose husband had been a prominent architect in Margate, a Kent seaside resort, and her daughter often gave genteel little dinner parties, assisted by their two maids. A menu that still survives features oysters, mutton cutlets and pheasant.

The only thing lacking in Christiana's life was romance. At forty-three, a tall, stately woman whom people found a little intense, her expectations could not have been high. But she hadn't given up hope. Whenever gentlemen were present, even married gentlemen, her colour would rise, her laugh would become a little louder, and she would make sure they knew she was only thirty-four. It was a simple mistake, really, just a reversal of the numbers.

And then Dr. Beard came into her life. He was vigorous and reasonably handsome, and the fact that he had a wife and young family did not deter Christiana for a moment: she knew he was as smitten as she was. Women in the Victorian age were almost expected to be ill as a sign of refinement, so it was no big thing for Christiana to invent abdominal pains and persistent headaches as excuses to visit the intriguing doctor who thought nothing of prescribing opium-based laudanum, the aspirin of that day.

Soon, she was composing long and sensual love letters

to him in which she spoke of 'long kisses,' signing herself, 'Dorothea.' Dr. Beard, if he'd had any sense, would have tossed them in the waste. basket or, at the very least, told his wife about Miss Edmunds's foolish fancy. Instead, flattered by the letters that addressed him as 'Caro Mio,' and referred derisively to his wife as 'La Sposa,' he foolishly replied to them. Perhaps he thought of it as an elaborate game. He couldn't have been more mistaken. His less-than-effusive replies were all that Christiana needed to convince her of his passion. All that stood in the way of their happiness now was Mrs. Beard.

There is no evidence to show where Christiana bought the chocolates or where she procured the poison on that first occasion. But, in March 1871, she paid a social call on the unsuspecting doctor's wife. After a chat in the drawing room, she offered Mrs. Beard a chocolate, playfully putting it into her hostess's mouth. Mrs. Beard bit into it, then, forgetting her manners, spat most of it out, declaring it was 'horrible.' It must have been a bad one, suggested Christiana, and urged her to try another. Mrs. Beard declined.

After her guest had left, Mrs. Beard had pains in her stomach and was nauseous. She found it difficult to believe Miss Edmunds had actually tried to poison her, but finally she shared her suspicions with her husband. Dr. Beard, of course, understood at once why Christiana had done it, but he faced a dilemma. If he informed the police, his romantic correspondence with his patient would come to light and cause a scandal. After due consideration, Dr. Beard took the cautious and, as it turned out, fatal route. He saw Christiana, told her of

216

his suspicions and said he had no wish to see her again, socially or as a patient.

As the door closed behind him, Christiana threw herself on the chaise lounge. How could she live without seeing her beloved doctor again? She had told him his suspicions were totally unfounded, but he hadn't believed her. How could she convince him he was wrong? Then an idea came to her. If she could show the Beards that there was a poisoner loose in Brighton, and that it was not she who had tampered with the chocolates, they would have to apologize and welcome her into their home again. She could just imagine that joyful moment.

Her first step was to call at Maynard's, one of Brighton's best-known confectioners, on West Street, demanding to see the owner. She told John Goddard Maynard, who had operated the business for more than twenty-five years and who was nearly blind, that she had bought some chocolate creams from his shop for a friend and that they had made her ill. 'A gentleman friend of mine intends to have them analysed,' she said. Maynard was shocked. 'I wish you would have them analysed,' he told her. 'I am sure they are all right. I've never had a complaint before.' And to prove his confidence, he took one of the suspect chocolate creams from the jar on the counter and ate it in her presence.

Shortly afterwards, Isaac Garrett, a pharmacist on Queen's Row, was packaging up some toilet articles for a woman customer he knew by sight but not by name when she asked him out of the blue if he would sell her some strychnine. She needed it to get rid of some cats that were digging up seeds in her garden, she explained.

217

Strychnine was a horribly painful way to get rid of cats, suggested Garrett, and besides, it was dangerous to have poison around the house.

'But my husband and I have no children. There is no danger of an accident,' she replied. In any case, he said, he couldn't sell poison without having a witness to attest to the identity of the purchaser in his poison book.

The woman looked thoughtful as she left. The bell over the door tinkled as she entered the milliner's shop three doors up the street. She was looking for a 'Shetland fall,' a type of shawl popular at that time, she told the milliner, Caroline Stone. After picking one out and paying for it, she said, as if as an afterthought, 'Oh, I wonder if you could do me a favour. My husband and I are naturalists and we use strychnine in our work. I have to buy some at Mr. Garrett the chemist's, but I need someone to sign the book for me. Just a formality really.'

Mrs. Stone said it would be no trouble at all, and a few minutes later she signed the book, affirming that the purchaser was indeed 'Mrs. Wood, of Hillside, Kingston.' Miss Edmunds left the store with a white paper bag in her purse containing ten grains of strychnine. A quarter of a grain is enough to kill an adult, and half that will finish a child.

Christiana Edmunds then became a student of the habits and routines of small boys. She finally settled on Adam May, a bright-looking eleven-year-old, as one of her accomplices, stopping him one day on King Street and asking him if he would do an errand for her. Polite little Adam listened as she explained that she wanted him to go to Maynard's and buy sixpennyworth of large

218

chocolate creams. A few minutes later, he was back with them. His employer opened the bag, but said they were not the sort she wanted. She sent him back to Maynard's, where Adam watched the girl behind the counter pour them back into the jar before giving him some smaller ones. These, the strange lady said, were the right ones and, taking a larger piece of chocolate cream from a piece of paper in her hand, she gave it to him as a reward.

Several other boys were stopped on the street by the tall, fashionably-dressed lady and asked to go through the same peculiar routine of fetching chocolates from Maynard's and then returning them. Finally, the staff became suspicious, and an assistant actually followed one of the boys and saw him give the chocolates to a woman he later identified as Christiana Edmunds.

Garrett, the pharmacist, was surprised to see 'Mrs. Wood' back in his shop on April 15, barely two weeks after her original strychnine purchase. The poison had had no effect on the cats so far, she complained, and she wanted more. She bought another ten grains, getting Mrs. Stone to sign the poison book, this time buying a veil from the milliner. A month later, the woman came in for more poison, this time claiming she and her husband were moving and needed it to put down an old dog.

By June, the cat and dog stories were wearing thin. Miss Edmunds's next ploy, again making use of her team of young messengers, showed rare cunning. On June 9, a small boy presented himself to Mr. Garrett with a note supposedly from Messrs. Glaisyer and Kemp, a drugstore on North Street. They had run short of strychnine, said the note, and would be obliged if Garrett would send them

219

a quarter of an ounce in a sealed bottle. He could trust the boy to bring it. Garrett instead sent back a note asking if a drachm – about 60 grains – would be enough. Any suspicions he had were dispelled when the boy returned with half a crown and another note saying that would be plenty.

Christiana Edmunds was obviously lacing a lot of chocolates with poison that spring, likely using her skill with a sewing needle to introduce the strychnine; the great mystery is that people weren't dropping like flies. It says little for the quality of Maynard's chocolates that no one complained, although later a number of people claimed they had become ill after eating them. Now all that was about to change.

In June, Charlie Miller, a coachbuilder from Hammersmith, in London, was holidaying in Brighton with his sister and brother-in-law, Mr. and Mrs. Albert Barker, and their four-year-old son, Sidney. On June 12, wanting to play the genial guest, he bought a shilling's worth of chocolate creams at Maynard's. After eating two or three himself, he felt dizzy and noticed a coppery taste in his mouth. Worse, his limbs began to stiffen. He recovered, and his brother-in-law tasted one of the chocolates, but spat it out, declaring it tasted too coppery. To the growing list of imbeciles who made possible the ensuing tragedy – Dr. Beard, who kept quiet; Garrett, who doled out poison like penny candies; Maynard, who failed to take the poison warning seriously – must now be added Albert Barker. After seeing what the chocolates did to Charlie, and even after trying one himself, he still gave one to little Sidney after dinner. Within ten minutes, the boy began to cry. His mother took him in her arms, and a surgeon, Mr. Richard Rugg, was sent for. By the time he arrived a few minutes later, the boy was in convulsions; eight minutes later he was dead.

An inquest was opened and then adjourned. A few days later, Garrett was surprised to see little Adam Smith, who had carried away the 60 grains of strychnine, peering over his counter once again. This time he had a note, ostensibly from the coroner, David Black, saying that he wished to examine Garrett's poison book in connection with the Barker inquest. A few minutes later, Adam put the book, now wrapped in paper, in Miss Edmunds's hands and was rewarded with a chocolate that went down a treat. When the book was returned to him a few days later, Garrett noticed a page had been torn out. But this time, Miss Edmunds had slipped up. She had torn out the wrong page. When the book was examined later, the 'Mrs. Wood' signatures were found and identified as being in her handwriting. At the resumed inquest, Miss Edmunds created a minor sensation when she volunteered under oath that she had bought some chocolate creams at Maynard's the previous September, pink and white ones, and felt ill after tasting only two. 'I had a violent internal pain and burning in the throat,' she reported. 'I took some brandy, which made me worse.' In March, undeterred, she had bought some more, she claimed, but after tasting one, she noticed a metallic flavour. 'My throat felt burning hot and I was strange all over,' she said. A lady friend to whom she had given one (presumably Mrs. Beard) had experienced the same symptoms.

The verdict of accidental death brought in by the jury

was a disappointment to Miss Edmunds. Hadn't they listened to her? Didn't they realize there was a maniac loose, trying to poison good people like herself? In the following days, Albert Barker received three anonymous letters from people signing themselves 'An old inhabitant and seeker for justice,' 'C.G.B.' and 'A London trades man now a visitor at Brighton.' Each letter urged him to take civil action against Maynard's. 'No parent could let the loss of his child be passed over in this cursory way,' said one letter. An expert would identify the writing in each of the letters as belonging to Christiana Edmunds.

Today, when even a hint that baby food has been tampered with results in massive recalls by manufacturers, we can only wonder that during that spring and summer no one seemed to be worrying about Brighton's poisoned chocolates. Harriet Cole, the wife of a grocer on Church Street, would report that after Miss Edmunds visited her store she found a bag of chocolate creams. Her daughter and a friend had become sick after eating them. Several months later she found another bag of chocolates and lemon bull's-eyes after Miss Edmunds had been in. Her daughter tried one of the chocolates and spat it out. There upon Mrs. Cole kindly gave the remainder to a little boy named Walker who took them home to his mother; she was ill the whole day after tasting one and declared she had never felt so strange before or since.

Two teenage boys would say they were in Spring Gardens when Miss Edmunds gave them a bag of chocolate creams that made them both ill, while pretty little Emily Baker was sick for two days after a kind lady gave her chocolates as she was coming out of school. A week later Miss Edmunds called at Emily's home to inquire if anyone had been sick in that house.

At this point Christiana's little campaign entered its second phase. Prominent people around town, including the editor of the *Gazette*, began receiving mysterious food parcels in the mail containing goodies that sometimes made them ill. Some bore Brighton postmarks; others came from London. Inside there was usually a friendly, but unsigned note. 'A few home-made cakes for the children,' said one. 'Those done up are flavoured on purpose for you to enjoy.' Miss Edmunds complained twice to the police that she had received such parcels. On the second occasion, Police Inspector Gibbs called at the Gloucester Place house and found Christiana lying on a couch and looking pale.

'Here I am again, Mr. Gibbs, nearly poisoned,' she greeted him in a faint voice. 'You have heard I had a box sent to me with some it in it?' He nodded. 'It came on Thursday evening in the post.' What was in it? Some strawberries, which her mother had eaten with no ill effects. But when Christiana had tried an apricot from the parcel it had been bitter and she had spat it out. Inspector Gibbs went away, thinking his own thoughts.

He was back again on August 17 with a warrant for the arrest of Christiana Edmunds, charging her with attempting to poison Mrs. Beard, the doctor's wife. Dr. Beard had finally shared his suspicions with the police.

'*I* poison Mrs. Beard!' declared Christiana on being charged. 'Who can say so? I've been nearly poisoned myself.'

By the time Christiana Edmunds appeared in the dock

at the Old Bailey in London, on January 15, 1872, she was charged with the murder of Sidney Albert Barker, aged four. The prisoner, wearing black velvet trimmed with fur, showed remarkable composure, studying the faces in the ladies' gallery before settling down with a quill in her gloved hand to make notes as Mr. Sergeant Ballantine commenced his opening address for the prosecution.

The facts were incontrovertible. As her legion of young messengers took their places, one after another, in the witness box; after Garrett the pharmacist; Maynard the confectioner; F.G. Nethercliffe, a hand-writing expert; the mothers of poisoned children; and the relatives of Sidney Barker all gave their evidence, there was no doubt at all about her guilt. Only once did Miss Edmunds register emotion: when Dr. Beard took the stand, she blushed scarlet.

It was not until the second day of the trial that the true facts behind the Edmunds's genteel existence on Gloucester Place emerged. Mrs. Ann Edmunds, Christiana's mother, was sobbing even before she gave her evidence. When she had regained some sort of control, she told the court that her husband, the architect who designed Trinity Church and other landmarks in Margate, had become insane in 1843 and was admitted to a private asylum for a year when, because of the heavy expense, he had had to come home.

'He would rave about having millions,' she said. 'On one occasion he tried to knock down our family doctor with a ruler. He had to be put in a straitjacket.' In 1845, he was confined in the Peckham Lunatic Asylum where, after becoming paralysed, he died two years later.

There had been a son, Arthur Burn Edmunds, who had been subject to epileptic fits from childhood. He had become increasingly violent and, in February 1860, when they could no longer manage him, he had been taken to Earlswood Asylum where he died six years later. A daughter too, Christiana's sister, had shown signs of insanity and had once tried to throw herself from a window. She had died at age thirty-six.

The courtroom was completely still as Mrs. Edmunds exposed secrets so long concealed in this tragic family. Her father, a major in the army, had had to be strapped in a chair and was completely childish before he died in a fit at forty-three, she said. Eight years earlier, Christiana had become ill and was sent to London for care. 'When she came back,' said Mrs. Edmunds, 'she was paralysed on one side and in her feet.' A surgeon had treated her. 'She would come into my room at night and say she had had a fit of hysteria and could not breathe.'

Mrs. Edmunds had been full of apprehension as her daughter approached the age at which her husband became insane. 'She is so like her father,' she said. Her fears increased when, after meeting Dr. Beard, 'I noticed a great change in her demeanour.' After Dr. Beard accused her of trying to poison his wife, 'she went around the room quite mad.' Had Mrs. Edmunds spoken to anyone about the possibility that her daughter was unbalanced? She shook her head, and her reply was almost inaudible: 'It was a delicate subject to speak of.'

A chaplain at the Lewes Jail, where Christiana had been held, testified that, when asked about the poisonings, she

225

broke into an extraordinary laugh and then into tears. 'She is on the borderline between crime and insanity,' said Dr. Charles Robertson, a specialist in mental illness. The judge, Sir Samuel Martin, Baron of the Exchequer, had little patience with this talk of insanity. Strange, he said, how poor people charged with crimes were rarely described as insane, 'but it is common to raise a defence of that kind when people of means are charged.' It was not the jury's duty to speculate on whether the insanity of her father had had any effect upon Miss Edmunds, he said, but to decide simply whether she had known right from wrong.

Christiana had told one of her doctors she would rather be found guilty than insane. She got her wish. It took the jury an hour to find her guilty. As Baron Martin prepared to put on the black cap to sentence her to death, Christiana finally spoke. 'It is owing to my having been a patient of his [Dr. Beard's],' she said, 'and the treatment I received in going to him that I have been brought into this dreadful business. I wish,' she said, yearning in her voice, 'that the jury had known the intimacy, his affection for me, and the way I have been treated.'

Asked in the customary way after sentence had been passed if there was anything in her condition as a woman to prevent it being carried out, she replied that she was pregnant. The sensation was short-lived. One of the several doctors in court examined her and reported she was not expecting a child.

The verdict and sentence aroused outrage in some quarters: 'If this wretched, half-crazed creature, the sister, daughter and grandchild of lunatics, is put out of the world in deference to a judicial definition of the plea of insanity,' editorialized the *Daily Telegraph* 'her death will bring disgrace upon British justice.' The appeal to the government's humane instincts prevailed: Christiana Edmunds's death sentence was commuted to committal to the Broadmoor Asylum for the Criminally Insane, where she lived on, forgotten by all except her intimates.

Wilhelm Kuhe, a Brighton pianist and impresario, happened to attend a Christmas ball at the institution in the 1890s. 'The figure I most vividly remember,' he related later, 'was that of one of the inmates, a tall woman of more than middle age who, while dancing, suddenly caught sight of me and stared hard at me again and again as she waltzed with her partner round the ballroom. When the dance was finished she came straight up to me. "You are Mr. Wilhelm Kuhe," she said. "I am," I replied, looking into her face and observing that it was powdered and painted to an extent that was disgusting. "You don't remember me?" she said with a ghastly smile: her mouth appeared to have been contorted as if by paralysis. I had to admit I did not. "Have you forgotten all the excitement there was over Christiana Edmunds?" she asked.'

The one person who, of course, did not forget Christiana was her mother. Faithfully, every six months, Ann Edmunds would make her way to the asylum. There a tea tray would be brought to the governor's study as a special concession to the family's social position, and mother and daughter would chat amiably about the weather and about the Queen's health and such, just as if they were still entertaining back in Gloucester Terrace.

Christiana was seventy-nine when she died in Broadmoor in 1907.

OUT OF
THE WINDOW

Our final destination is Winnipeg to learn about the involvement of a seemingly ordinary woman named Katie Harper in a most extraordinary murder. Katie, like several woman in this book, simply drifted into murder without, I am certain, giving it much thought. And, not untypically, she acted under the influence of a man.

It's a June night in the Winnipeg suburb of Old St. James; endless prairie winter is over and, with no pause for spring, summer rushes in. The sound of music drifts through open windows; cigarette tips glow on porches as people take a last drag before going to bed. On Parkhill Street, lights in the one-and-a-half-storey insulbrick houses go out one by one, leaving the night to the rasping crickets.

Then, at number 312, a different sound: a scraping, a thumping as a large object falls from the dormer window, rolls down the steep roof and drops to the concrete path below with a thud. There is no cry, no scream. But Leading Aircraftsman John Down, twenty-four, lies naked and dead on the path, his head in the flowerbed.

'He used to climb out on the roof for a cigarette,' his wife, Katie, tells the police. 'He must have slipped. Or maybe he was sleepwalking. He did that too.'

The autopsy showed Down had taken a large amount of sodium amytal, a sleepingpill. Nothing surprising about that. Before leaving work that day he had told friends he hadn't been sleeping well and meant to get a good night's sleep. John Down, a coroner's jury decided, died of an overdose.

Katie took his body back the thousands of miles to Newfoundland, where he had grown up. Funny though, thought John's sister, Sylvia, at the time, Katie didn't seem a bit upset. Others at the funeral were overwrought. 'Here,' said Katie, a nurse, as she handed around some little capsules. 'These might help.' They were sodium amytal, and Sylvia put one of them away in a trunk.

At the *Winnipeg Tribune*, John MacLean, one of the biggest scamps and wiliest reporters it's ever been my privilege to know, marched into managing editor Eric Wells's office and plunked down an article he'd written. 'Hang on to that,' he said. 'Some day it'll happen, and then you can run this story.' The article announced that Katie Down and her boyfriend, Sandy Harper, had just been charged with the murder of John Down. That was in 1959, and Wells carefully stored away MacLean's story.

Time passed: in 1960 Katie married Sandy Harper, who was an orderly at the Deer Lodge Hospital where she also worked. Two children were born to them in addition to the two Katie had by Down. Then, in 1976, after sixteen years of marriage, Katie and Sandy separated. That year a fellow called Douglas Shelmerdine, the common-law husband of Katie's daughter, Daphne, went to the police with stories he'd heard from his mother-in-law when she'd been drinking. John Down, she'd told him, was actually murdered by Sandy Harper. Shelmerdine got five hundred dollars for his tip-off, and Katie got the third degree and a lie-detector test from the police.

The story she told them – and which stood up under the lie-detector test – was that Sandy had come to the house on Parkhill Street late on that fatal evening and had made sexual advances. 'John's asleep upstairs,' she'd told him. 'I'll fix that,' he said. She followed him upstairs, mesmerized.

In the little slope-sided bedroom, she said, Sandy took a pillow and pressed it down on John Down's face until he stopped struggling. Didn't she cry out? Protest? No, she followed him back downstairs where 'he as much as raped me.' It was only then that they returned to the bedroom and, with her helping – a nurse and an orderly, they were used to shifting bodies – he shoved Down out of the window. 'I will never forget the thud as long as I live when he hit the sidewalk,' she told the cops.

Finally, Katie Harper felt she was emerging from the nightmare. What she called seventeen years of hell living with the violent Sandy were over. Having told her story, she waited confidently for the police to arrest him for murder. Yes, she'd told them, she was willing to testify against her former husband.

231

But Harper was no fool. He refused to talk. He refused a lie-detector test. There was no evidence placing him in the Down house that night. What were the police to do? They had a murder on their hands, an investigation that had earlier been botched, and two suspects, on one of whom they couldn't pin a thing. They did the obvious thing: they charged Katie Harper with murder and, in 1978, never a beauty, her features now harsh, deeply lined, she went on trial – alone.

Covering the trial in Winnipeg's gloomy grey marble Number One courtroom at the law-courts building was a young English-born correspondent for *Maclean's* magazine named Peter Carlyle-Gordge. Listening to the prosecution evidence, he assumed Katie Harper was guilty, that at the very least she had taken part in the murder of her first husband. Otherwise – and this continued to bother him even after he came to a different view of the case – why had she married Harper the year after the murder and stayed with him all that time?

Cletus A'Hearne, by then a retired Royal Canadian Mounted Police corporal who had investigated Down's death back in 1959, told the court, 'I wasn't satisfied ten minutes after I was on the scene that this man had jumped and died.' He didn't have far to look for a suspect. Katie, he said, had struck him at the time as 'an unimpressive, unattractive woman, unkempt in appearance, callous and deceitful.' Would A'Hearne have regarded her differently, we wonder, if she had been pert and pretty?

Katie Harper's statement, given to police right after she completed the polygraph test, was admitted as evidence. In it, she swore that she had given Down three sodium amytal capsules when he asked for them before going to bed. Then, a courtroom shocker: the polygraph technician testified that, after taking the test, Katie had told him she had actually slipped the three capsules into her husband's coffee that night. That capsule stored by John Down's sister all those years was entered as an exhibit, and essentially the prosecution case wrapped up with a neighbour testifying she had seen Sandy Harper stripped to the waist in the Downs' kitchen one night while John was still alive.

Amazingly, the defence called no witnesses. The jury did not hear Katie Harper's account of what happened that night in her own words, leaving the way open for the prosecutor, George Dangerfield, to describe her as 'a cold-blooded, ruthless killer' who, wanting to get rid of her husband, slipped as many as seven or eight capsules into his coffee, smothered him and, unaided, heaved his body out of the window. The jury bought the theory, and Katie, then forty-four, was sentenced to life imprisonment with no possibility of parole until 2003. Carlyle-Gordge rounded off his account for *Maclean's* with the kind of ironic touch any journalist treasures: Katie had worked for the last ten years as an embalmer at a local funeral home.

But Cathy Carlyle-Gordge, his wife, who was a public-relations officer with the Winnipeg Health Services Centre, had doubts. 'I was once prescribed sodium amytal,' she said. 'It was the most foul, bitter, terrible-tasting stuff. You could never slip it into someone's coffee.' Peter got a message from his office in Toronto

233

that Shelmerdine, Katie's son-in-law, wanted to see him. He got distinctly nervous when Shelmerdine, experiencing a bad case of nerves himself, met him at the door, waving a gun. 'He sounded very weird,' recalled Peter. The son-in-law was feeling pangs of guilt. He'd acted as a paid police informer, but his tip-off had completely misfired: his mother-in-law rather than Sandy Harper had gone down for the murder. But why, asked Peter, had Katie married Sandy if he was a murderer? 'Because he threatened to kill her if she ever told,' said Shelmerdine. As his wife, Katie would not be able to testify against him, Sandy assumed.

How could Peter be sure Shelmerdine wasn't making it all up? Well once, he said, Katie had arranged for him and a friend, Irven Derksen, to hide outside her kitchen window while she got Sandy to talk about the murder. They'd heard Sandy say, 'If you say anything about it (Down's death) I will kill you too.'

Peter and Cathy Carlyle-Gordge became Winnipeg's version of Tommy and Tuppence Beresford, Agatha Christie's young fictional detective couple. More and more of their time − and eventually their money − was given over to tracking down possible witnesses to prove Katie Harper's innocence. It took them a year to find Irven Derksen, who, by then, was working on an oil rig in Alberta. Yes, he remembered Sandy making the threat exactly as Shelmardine had described it.

Just as John MacLean had done so many years before, they contacted the Downs' neighbours on Parkhill Street and found that Katie's kitchen that night had been, as Peter put it, 'like Grand Central station.' There was a

234

steady stream of people dropping by for coffee and a chat, and several heard John snoring upstairs. When the last one left — before Sandy Harper arrived — Katie was calmly washing the dishes. It hardly seemed the scenario for a murder conspiracy. Sandy's first wife, Rose, whom he had divorced in order to marry Katie, told of an alcoholic husband, abusive and cruel toward his family and with a police record for violence.

Finally, and with some apprehension, they went to visit Katie in the Portage-la-Prairie correctional centre. The woman who took a seat opposite them in the prison library turned out to be not at all like the 'callous and deceitful' person A'Hearne had described. Shy and restrained at first, she soon showed herself to be a warm and affectionate person, a model prisoner to whom the younger inmates brought their troubles. They called her 'Mom.'

As Peter and Cathy gained her confidence, she told them of her strict Mennonite upbringing in a small Saskatchewan town and of having to leave when she became pregnant in her teens. After her first lover was killed on leave from war service in Korea, she started dating John Down, who was with the Royal Canadian Air Force, and they eventually married and moved to Winnipeg, where they had two daughters. But her husband, she said, became increasingly homesick for his native Newfoundland, was subject to outbursts of temper and periods of depression and was demanding sex up to three or four times a day. Katie was already having an affair with an orderly at the hospital where she worked when she met Sandy.

But still, she insisted, she did not murder her husband, although she admitted she had helped dispose of his body by lifting his legs to push him through the window. After Sandy left that night, she had run out with a coat to cover Down's naked body and then had gone to a neighbour's to give the alarm. Why hadn't she gone to the police earlier? The inquest finding – that Down had died of an overdose – prevented that, she claimed. As a nurse she would have had access to drugs, so she would have been pointing the finger at herself if she claimed he was murdered. And, too, there were Sandy's threats.

'Frankly,' said Cathy, 'we were trying to trip her up.'

'But when we checked out her statements they all tended to be true,' said Peter. One day, he said, he would believe her guilty, the next he would swing right around and be convinced of her innocence. The couple had endless debates with friends, arguing, in turn, for her innocence or guilt, as if they were in court.

Then they made up their minds. Going way beyond his role as disinterested journalist, Peter filed an affidavit with the Manitoba Court of Appeal, suggesting that the evidence about Katie's putting sodium amytal capsules into the coffee was implausible. As a result, Katie eventually won a new trial. It wasn't the time to hold back: Cathy put up their Winnipeg home as surety so that Katie could be released on bail, and she came to stay with them.

When Katie stood trial again in the same courtroom early in 1982, Sandy Harper, now a skinny, beaten-looking man of sixty-four, was in the dock beside her, also charged with murder. And this time, too, Katie got some of the breaks when a police toxicologist, William Radych, admitted that only four days earlier he had discovered that, in his original analysis in 1959, he had made a simple mathematical error in calculating the amount of barbiturate in the body. The corrected figures suggested Down had received only a normal therapeutic dose, enough to help him to sleep.

This time a son and daughter by Sandy's first marriage remembered their father coming home one night, sobbing and telling their mother, Rose, 'I' or 'we' had killed a man. In the witness box, Rose recalled that, even when he was divorcing her, Sandy had said she was prettier than Katie, whom he was marrying. And just before the wedding – when the police heat was off – he even offered to forget about marrying Katie and resume their relationship, clearly suggesting he was marrying Katie to keep her quiet.

A not-very-pretty picture emerged of Sandy as Katie's daughters took the witness stand. Kathy confirmed that he had sexually molested her for years, while Sherry, fathered by Sandy, told how she would urinate in the wastebasket in her bedroom rather than risk meeting her brutal father on the way to the bathroom. But, she said, 'when my mother comes into the room it's like the sun coming out from behind the clouds.'

'The years with my mother,' testified daughter Daphne 'were beautiful. She always softened the blows.'

Because co-accused can't testify against each other, this was to be a complicated and difficult trial. If Sandy had been able to give his version – which was that, when he arrived at Katie's that night, her husband was already nearly dead from the barbiturates, and that he had only helped push him out of the window – and Katie had been able to tell hers, jurors could have made up their own minds whom to believe. As it was, they had to find their way through a fog of suspicion and oblique accusations. And, just as in the first trial, when the polygraph technician's out-of-the-blue testimony proved so important, in this one a wild-card witness appeared, and all bets were off.

The prosecutor, George Dangerfield, interrupted the defence to say he had a surprise witness he wished to call. An older woman entered the witness box and identified herself as Sister Norma Lillian Johnson, a nun belonging to the order of the Sisters of Our Lady of Charity. While visiting Katie in prison, she said, she had 'the impression' that Katie had confessed to the murder and that she had said she would do it again. Her evidence caused an uproar. A Roman Catholic monsignor announced publicly that Johnson was not a member of any recognized Catholic order and had no right to call herself a Roman Catholic nun, but by then the damage was done. After deliberating for eight hours, the jury found Katie guilty of first-degree murder and Sandy guilty of second-degree murder. Both received life sentences.

There were ample grounds for appeals, perhaps too many. Chief Justice Samuel Freedman, confronted by what had now become a legal mare's nest, decided, instead of ordering new trials, to reduce both convictions to manslaughter. The defence lawyers and their clients breathed easier. Manslaughter — which Down's death clearly wasn't — usually involved a sentence of two to three years. With the time she'd already served, Katie would walk free. Instead, when the time came for sentencing, they both received twenty years.

'We were shattered,' said Peter Carlyle-Gordge. 'It broke our spirits.' The book he was writing about the case was supposed to end with Katie being exonerated and winning her freedom. Now he has abandoned the book. After giving four years of their lives and more than ten thousand dollars to the case, Peter and Cathy left Winnipeg with their children. When I spoke to them on a mild January day they were living in Bexhill-on-sea, a popular retirement spot on the south coast of England. 'I tried to forget the whole thing,' said Peter, as the children played with their pet rabbit on the lush grass outside the window.

After the initial depression they were able to look at the case more objectively. Was Katie Harper guilty? 'Morally, if not legally, she was guilty,' said Peter. 'I don't think she ever planned this murder, but she made her big mistake in not going to the police.'

'As a woman, I can understand that,' said Cathy. 'She was absolutely terrified that Sandy would kill her children. He'd told her, 'If I don't do it, someone else will.'

The couple saw Katie in 1987 when she got a four-day leave from prison. 'She was the happiest I had ever seen her,' said Cathy. In 1988, she was released on parole and went to live with one of her daughters on the West Coast. At Christmas, the Carlyle-Gordges had received

239

a card from her. 'If you wrote it all as a novel,' said Peter as I left, 'no one would believe you.'

And John MacLean? He never got to enjoy his triumph. Broke, out of work and coping with a perennial drinking problem and a heart condition, he hanged himself ten days before Christmas, 1977. He was fifty-four and he was a legend in his time.